ON THE OTHER SIDE OF THE DOOR

By Mark Huling

Printed in the United States of America

ISBN 978-1-98080971-5

Cover Photograph by Robert Inglis

Contents

ON THE OTHER SIDE OF THE DOOR

By Mark Huling

AUTHOR'S NOTE

Throughout history there has always been a mystique surrounding mental illness and the methods used to treat people suffering from it. From the beginning of recorded history there have been attempts made not only to help these people, but to figure out why they are afflicted. Mental illness has been mistaken for many things, including demonic possession. In the past many were treated inhumanely and cruelly. Psychiatry was born out of the need to explain and understand the human mind. To this day many aspects of mental illness remain a mystery. The advent of modern day psychiatric drugs has greatly helped in the treatment of many individuals, but the "Science" remains an ongoing struggle.

This story takes place between 1972 and 1978. It is based on the years that I worked as a psychiatric technician at Camarillo State Hospital in Southern California. Most of the people and events I describe are real. To protect the anonymity of certain characters in the book I will use only fictitious names or just first names unless it is a matter of public record. I apologize for any inaccuracies in the following content, as I relied mainly on my memory while writing these accounts. It was my intention to write about how I perceived my experiences there and to give the reader a glimpse into the way things really were on the other side of the door.

PROLOGUE

Its 6:15 on a cold January morning. My eyes are shut tight. The alarm clock goes off making a most obscene noise. I struggle to turn it off as I begin to realize it is time to get up. My young wife lying next to me is muttering something like "You'd better get up or you will be late for work again" as she buries her head in the pillows. I'm thinking to myself that I had one too many beers the night before but just suck it up and get your ass in gear. I race through my morning rituals and climb into my car a little before seven. I turn on the heater and the defroster and after a couple of minutes I back out of the driveway of my microscopic duplex at the beach. It is about a half an hour drive on the freeway to my destination. I turn on the rock and roll radio station in my little Honda Civic and light up a cigarette.

I exit the freeway and drive along a two lane road for about three miles. I'm quite awake by now and I start thinking about my day ahead. I put my signal on and turn onto an even smaller two lane road that winds its way around the landscape like a slithering snake. It is flanked by tall Eucalyptus trees and prickly pear cactus with mountains on one side and farm fields on the other. I slow down as I approach the reduced speed sign ahead. I slowly drive through the old Spanish style stucco buildings and arrive in my designated parking lot hidden from the main road behind tall white concrete walls.

I get out of my car and light up another cigarette. I'm simply dressed in Levis, a T-shirt and boots with my heavy winter jacket on. I have shoulder length brown hair and stand about six feet tall. As I stride toward the entrance of my building a heavy ring of keys jingle on my side as I walk. I walk down a long hallway and stop at a doorway with only a small little window near the top of it. Reaching down to the keys hanging from my belt I grab an insanely large key that looks like it should unlock the door to a medieval castle. I take a deep breath and I insert the huge skeleton key into the old metal lock on the door and turn it until it clicks.............

CHAPTER 1
Getting There

I think I was always the kind of person who had the ability to look deep inside of things. From an early age I began asking questions about the nature of things, the nature of the universe. I remember my dad saying to me "Son, you are going to grow up to be a great philosopher someday". Well I never became that great philosopher but I have pondered many things and I have seen many things. Now that I have lived a big chunk of my life I can look back and easily second guess many of the decisions I made. I wonder how things might have turned out if I had just done some of them differently. Of course we all do that, don't we? The decision to become a psychiatric technician and to work in a mental hospital at such a young age definitely changed my life. The situations and events that I was directly exposed to during my six years there will be forever engrained in my mind.

My name is Mark. I grew up in the Midwest and moved to California at the age of eleven with my family. That was quite a major change for a young, impressionable boy like me. I never looked back. I graduated from high school in 1970 and like so many of my friends I had no idea what I wanted to do. I did know that I wanted to go to college and possibly earn a degree. I also thought about going to a technical school and learning a trade. I just wasn't sure.

That summer, after graduation, several of my buddies decided to enlist in the military. The Vietnam War was raging on and the draft was still in place. I remember talking to my best friend from across the street, who was enlisting in the Air Force, and asking him why he decided to do that. He told me that it was better than being drafted and that they promised him he would have a choice of where he was stationed. Well, I had to give that some major thought. I certainly didn't want to get drafted and sent to the jungles of Vietnam but I didn't want to enlist either. So I took my chances.

As it went, after a couple of college deferments and my draft lottery number coming up in the high three hundreds, I never got drafted. Was it luck or was it fate? I wasn't going to worry about it. I was proud of my friends that did enlist just as I am proud of all the men and women who have served our country. The U.S. Military draft ended on January 27, 1973 about two years before the war in Vietnam ended. At the time it was speculated that Richard Nixon thought it would help him politically because of the large anti-war movement sweeping across the nation.

I remember talking to a guidance counselor at the local junior college and after some deliberation I decided to start my first year with a business major. I signed up for way too many units and had to drop a couple of classes just to keep up. I was even taking two night classes, which I hated. After I finished my first two semesters of college I just wasn't feeling like I was going in the right direction. I had heard some talk around school about the psychiatric technician program they were offering. It was just a little more than a one year program that didn't get you a degree but with your certificate of graduation it pretty much guaranteed a job in the psychiatric nursing field. I said "OK, I'm going to give this a shot". So I applied for the program and was accepted on the contingency that I complete College Algebra and College English before I could start. So after a summer semester to get those classes under my belt I started the Psych Tech program in the fall of 1972.

It was a grueling fifty-four weeks that lay ahead of me. At times I wasn't sure if I was going to finish. They really packed a lot into one year. It was divided between the classroom and the field. We took Anatomy and Physiology, pharmacology classes, nursing theory and practice and other related courses. We were taught all of the medical terminology and abbreviations as well as measurements and units. We had several psychology and psych related classes, learning all about Sigmund Freud, Pavlov's dogs, Maslow's hierarchy of needs and Carl Jung, the father of analytical psychology. The actual nursing part of it was similar to the training that a licensed vocational nurse would receive, perhaps a little less. We got our hands-on nursing training at two of the large hospitals in the county, County Medical and Saint John's Hospital. The psych training was done at many facilities throughout the county but the bulk of it, and probably the most important part of it, was done on the actual treatment units at Camarillo State Hospital. It was nice, however, to get exposure to the other facilities throughout the county so that we got a well-rounded view of the various treatment programs that were available. We visited a methadone clinic (very depressing), a children's orthopedic school, a private mental hospital, various board and care homes, plus the county mental health department including both in-patient and day treatment centers, the Ventura County Association for the Retarded and Atascadero State Hospital, as well as others.

Although each of the required courses had its own instructor, there was one woman, Merriam, who oversaw the entire program and monitored each student and their progress. She provided individual counseling to deal with each student's problems and needs. She was also our leader and chaperone on most of the field trips and was our supervisor for on-sight training locations. I will never forget her. She was a short, rather unattractive older woman who wore bright red lipstick, rouge on her cheekbones, polyester pantsuits and was moderately overweight. She had Bell's palsy, which is a condition that causes one side of the face to droop and sometimes the speech to slur, which caused her to talk out of one side of her mouth. Despite these drawbacks she was a tireless bulldog that did everything in her power to help us succeed. She was never seen without her thick black leather brief case, where she kept every pertinent bit of information she could possibly use to enhance our educational experience. With that said I must mention that fifty-three people started the program and only twelve graduated. Some dropped out for personal reasons and others left because they were shocked at what they saw. Needless to say that when we were initially taken onto some of the psych and developmentally disabled units it was a brand new experience that none of us had ever seen before.

At the end of that long and arduous year I graduated! It was a feeling of great relief for me. I was now an officially accredited pre-licensed psychiatric technician, hopefully with all of the training I would need to start this looming, new profession. I would still, however, have to pass a California State Board examination in order to get fully licensed. I naturally gravitated to Camarillo State Hospital in searching for my first real job. I could have looked elsewhere, such as a private hospital or facility, but I applied there because I was somewhat familiar with it already, having done much of my field training there. I had gained valuable experience while training on not only the adult psychiatric units but the children's units, geriatric units and developmentally disabled units as well. I had also heard that the state paid well and had great benefits. I found out that they hired pre-licensed psychiatric technicians or PLPT's as we were called. So in just couple of weeks after graduation I applied for a job there, along with most of the other eleven people with whom I graduated.

It didn't take long before I got a phone call for an interview with program 3A, which was a short term admissions program that treated adult males with a wide variety of psychiatric conditions. The interview was held in the assistant program director's office before a panel of three or four people. I must have done fairly well as I was offered a job at the conclusion of the interview and I of course accepted. I felt good about myself at that moment in time. I was only twenty years old, single, had just landed a good paying job and had my whole life ahead of me. I could sense that it may be very challenging at times but I wanted to jump in and get my feet wet as soon as possible.

I spent the next two weeks going through the orientation process at the hospital which consisted of filling out a ton of paperwork, talking to a lot of important people, getting a complete tour of the hospital, which was huge by the way, and getting a complete physical examination. I was then assigned to my home unit, Unit 77. They gave me a set of keys and told me to report for work the next day. I would spend a week or two on the day shift getting my initial orientation and then I was to be assigned to the PM shift or "evening" shift. Apparently new nursing personnel were almost always assigned to PM's or NOC's "night" shift before you could apply to work on the day shift.

Some people preferred the PM and night shifts as there was less hustle and bustle and there was a 5% payroll shift differential for evenings and a 10% for the NOC shift. However if you really wanted to advance yourself and become an integral part of the treatment team the day shift was where all the action was. I figured I could do my six month stint on the evening shift and then request to be transferred to the day shift; at least that is what I hoped for in the beginning. So there were the three eight hour shifts per day and everything was done in military time, so I had to quickly learn that 0900 was nine in the morning and 2100 was nine at night, etc.

Building where Unit 77 was as it looks today

My new unit was located in a cluster of buildings that not only contained the three units that made up our program but housed the intake and screening facility where all new patients went before being sent to a particular unit for treatment. A determination was made there by the admitting MD and a preliminary diagnosis made. All of the program offices, medical clinics, the lab, the pharmacy, X-ray, physical therapy, medical/surgical, the autopsy room and the morgue were all in that same big complex. The rest of the hospital was spread out over many acres of land. There were row after row of old Spanish/ Mediterranean architectural style white buildings with red tile roofs. There was an M.I. (mentally ill) side and a D.D. (developmentally disabled) side. Situated in and around these two main sides of the hospital were all of the satellite buildings and facilities that made up everything else. There was a research unit, the alcoholic units, the geriatric units, the children's units, the adolescent units, administration buildings, classrooms, a chapel, a gymnasium, a library, an Olympic size swimming pool, a movie theater, a bowling alley, a patient canteen, an employee dining room, the main kitchen and patient dining rooms, all of the maintenance buildings, the fire department, the security police, employee housing, a full time painting crew, a landscaping crew, a housekeeping staff, laundry rooms, medical records and the list goes on and on.

The hospital was opened in 1936 and had a maximum patient population of over seven thousand by 1957. At the time it was touted as the largest mental hospital this side of the Mississippi River. This large facility was located a few miles from the coastline about sixty miles north of Los Angeles and was tucked into the countryside, surrounded by rugged mountains and green farmlands. In the early days of the hospital it was almost self-sustaining and had its own dairy, and fields of farm fresh vegetables, all of which was maintained with the help of the patients themselves. This was thought to be excellent therapy for some of the patient population. By the time I got there in the 1970's the population had shrunk and most of the food was brought in from the outside, but it was still a very busy place. Camarillo State Hospital was the site of many ground breaking inroads in the treatment of schizophrenia, using a combination of drug therapy as well as traditional psychotherapies and group therapy techniques.

Photograph by Robert Inglis
View of hospital grounds as it appears today

Over the decades Camarillo State hospital underwent many changes and had to endure the whims of the state bureaucracy and the winds of politics. Depending on who the governor was at the time the state hospital system in California never knew from year to year if all of it or part of it would be funded. Although some state hospitals still remain open in California, Camarillo State hospital was closed permanently in 1997. Some say the closing was due to fiscal constraints and the trend toward shifting the financial burden from the state to the counties and others say it was because of the stigma of alleged abuse and neglect and the mysterious deaths of over 100 patients. Even though I wasn't there when it closed I believe that it was a combination of both of those things that caused the closing. Years later it became the campus of California State University Channel Islands.

So I began my new job, and this new chapter in my life, at this fabled institution at the end of 1973. The United States had seen many front page news events that year. Everyone who remembers the 1970's knows what a wild decade it was, and like the 60's before it, it was a decade of great change. The Watergate scandal consumed the news all that year. Nixon announced the Vietnam peace accord in January. The World Trade Center was dedicated in April and in the case of Roe V. Wade, the Supreme Court overturned the states' ban on abortion. "Dark Side of the Moon" was released in the U.S. in March, Secretariat won the Triple Crown in June. Billie Jean King defeated Bobby Riggs in the battle of the sexes in September and "The Exorcist" and "The Sting" both opened in theaters in December.

CHAPTER 2
A Shocking Beginning

Having been through the training program on several of the treatments units while going to school, and observing from my standpoint, I thought I had a basic idea what to expect when I started my new job. Almost everything that we were taught was still fresh in my head. In reality I didn't know Jack shit. Some things just can't be taught. I reported for work feeling a little nervous and somewhat apprehensive, naturally. I had been briefly introduced to some of the staff members during my orientation but, as I soon found out, there were so many more to get acquainted with. Some of them I would work with closely every day and others more intermittently. Everyone seemed to be very friendly to me on that first day. I got the feeling that they knew that this was all new to me and seemed very accommodating and reassuring.

Just as in all workplaces the staff changes, people come and go, and you develop relations with your co-workers. Some you automatically gravitate toward and others may be a little harder to work with. I realized after a couple of days that there was a definite hierarchy or pecking order built into the system. Although we were all considered professionals the nursing staff was like the glue that held everything together, the worker bees. If you had to go by a hierarchy it would be the nursing staff followed by the more professional titles; rec therapists, social workers, psychologists and finally the medical doctors and psychiatrists. The unit supervisor or U.S. had the ultimate authority over all nursing staff for all three shifts. Our unit had maybe four or five psych techs on the day shift, one or two nurses, one recreational therapist, two social workers, one psychologist and two psychiatrists. The pm and night shifts were usually staffed solely by psych techs with a shift lead. The minimum number of psych techs and/or nurses allowed under state hospital regulations was three per shift.

It must be noted that not all of the psychiatrists that I had the pleasure of working with over the years were true board certified ones. You can say that all board certified psychiatrists are M.D.'s but not the other way around. If a non-board certified M.D. was working in the capacity of a psychiatrist, he or she still had full and unquestioned authority in regards to prescribing medication and reaching a diagnosis and treatment plan for their patients. As I gained experience over a period of time I would come to realize that a good doctor would always reach out to his staff members for their opinions. Doctors with little or no previous experience in the field of psychiatry tended to heavily rely on us for advice and information.

As the hierarchy continued on up the ladder, the unit supervisor would answer to the assistant program directors who answered to the program director who answered to the hospital board of supervisors who answered to the hospital administrator. The hospital administrator would then answer to all of the higher powers in Sacramento until you got to the top rung, the governor of California. I remember one year while Ronald Reagan was the governor of California, we were in the middle of a severe drought and the grass all over the hospital grounds was very dry and brown. In an attempt to make the hospital more visually appealing to the governor, on one of his rare visits, the grass was sprayed with green dye. We all thought it was such a ridiculous waste of taxpayers' money at the time. I don't know what the governor thought about it. One thing is for sure, I learned that the people up in Sacramento, most of them never having set foot on a state hospital grounds, had absolutely no problem setting all of the guidelines, regulations, performance standards, and every other kind of rule while sitting behind a desk from afar. That was always one of the biggest complaints lodged by the unit staff members the entire time I worked there. It was fruitless to complain or try to get something changed because we got the same response from our unit supervisor every time. She would always say that she had brought it to the attention of the program directors and that they in turn would always say that their hands were tied, and that was just the way it was. It was bureaucracy in its purest form.

Some of the first people that I met that first week I have never forgotten. Each of them were interesting in their own way I suppose. There was Margaret Garrison, the unit supervisor, who was a middle aged woman with platinum white hair and black horned rim glasses. Her personality was like sour grapes and her demeanor was all business. She would sit in her office chair in the back of the nursing station and bark out orders to anyone that came within a few feet of her. The rest of the time she was on the phone talking to as many people as she could possibly bother in an eight hour shift. She was very scary to me at first but I learned how to tiptoe around her as well as I could. Everyone else did the same thing. She was the person that instilled in me something that changed my life permanently. After I was ten minutes late for work two days in a row she sat me down in front of her in her little sanctuary in the back of the nursing station and in no uncertain terms told me in a stern, loud voice, with her piercing eyes locked on me from behind those frames, that if I couldn't get to work on time she would basically make things very difficult for me. "Around here we don't come to work late, period! I don't care what your excuse is." I shrunk back in my chair and said, "I'm sorry Mrs. Garrison. I will not be late again." She replied, "You'd better not be!" At that point something clicked in my brain. I had this personal epiphany about responsibility and maturity and all of that kind of mind thought. Believe it or not I was never late again, ever. I carried that practice throughout the rest of my working life.

The day shift lead was Ron Wallace, a tall young black guy with a medium length afro who dressed very sharply. He was loud and raucous and seemed to get the attention of everyone around him. Even though disco had not really begun yet he could have easily passed for a black John Travolta in Saturday Night Fever. He was a total workaholic who ran around the unit like a Tasmanian devil on steroids. He was so focused on the matters at hand that he often forgot to drink water to keep himself hydrated. On more than one occasion he had to take time off work to recover from kidney infections as a result of it. He answered to Margaret Garrison but knew just how to handle her. He was a cool dude for sure. When there was time to shoot the breeze he would sometimes gather some of the guys around and proceed to tell us all about his incredible sexual prowess. Some of the situations he described with the ladies left us just shaking our heads in disbelief. From the very beginning I knew that I wanted to have the same drive and determination as Ron.

I owe much gratitude to many people who helped me out in those early days. Mary Baldwin was a psych tech who was the epitome of someone you might call an "Old Bughouser". She was near the end of her working life and had a lot of experience. She was very motherly in nature and seemed to take a special interest in me from the start. When you had a question she had an answer. She taught me how to dispense medication, how to give intramuscular and subcutaneous injections (we had only given a few shots during our nursing training), how to read doctor's orders and so much more. She was a kind and gentle soul but knew how to handle herself in a sometimes extremely tense environment.

Jean Winters was another great lady. She was probably in her mid-forty's, stood about five feet tall, and was a true team player. She was fearless. She also had been a psych tech for many years. I loved talking to her. She could go on and on about her daughters, and especially her husband, but when duty called she sprang into action. She also helped teach me essential things like charting, clinic scheduling, and many of the day to day routines and procedures on the unit.

There were Gill Smith and Terry Ferguson, two of the male techs that were there when I first started. Gil was in his forty's and kind of a non-descript guy who had a goatee and smoked a pipe. He had about six kids and a stay-at-home wife. He drove an old 1960's station wagon. Although he was a descent psychiatric technician, I got the feeling that his main concern, and the thing that motivated him the most, was to feed and clothe his family. He grabbed as much overtime as possible. Sometimes he would work thirty straight days, including many double shifts and even triple shifts. He slept in his station wagon in the parking lot of the unit in between shifts. Terry Ferguson was a spillover from the hippie generation. He was a short guy with shoulder length hair, a big bushy mustache and wore John Lennon style spectacles. He was kind of an asshole at times but always had your back.

There was Tim, the old cranky guy who walked the halls and bossed the patients around. I never understood what value he had as a staff member. There was Audrey Mason, the outgoing redhead technician in her late twenties and Amy Harris, a registered nurse that stood about 4'11".

Only a few psych techs or nurses chose to wear traditional hospital uniforms. We were not required to, so almost everyone wore street clothes. I was required to wear hospital greens during my training in traditional hospitals and was kind of surprised when I realized that everyone could dress as they pleased. Contrary to popular belief we did not wear those white uniforms that you see psychiatric nurses wearing in so many movies.

There were the two female social workers, Kathy and Rita who had their offices just across from the nursing station. Adjacent to their offices were two isolation rooms, or "side rooms" as we called them. These were not "padded rooms" as one might think. On the contrary they were small rooms with thick masonry walls and a little window in the door. A mattress and blanket were the only things in the room. During the first week I was there I remember hearing a loud scream coming from one of the social worker's office. We ran into her office to see a highly agitated man running around inside it as she clung to her desk in a self-preserving posture. He had been in the side room next to her office because he was exhibiting extreme psychotic symptoms and had been ordered to be in there by the doctor. It seems that he had bored a hole through the thick concrete-like wall and climbed through it into her office. We nicknamed him "Willie the Beaver" as his name was William.

Down the hall and heading toward the dining room was the recreational therapist's room. His name was Bob Rodriguez. At the other end of the hallway was Dr. Ellison's office. He was the unit psychologist. Dr. Ellison was a very interesting character. He got his PhD from Boston College and shortly thereafter took the job at Camarillo State Hospital. The first time I saw him he was running around the unit with a group of patients following him in what seemed like a frenzied mode, to say the least. He had wavy red hair and a scraggly beard. I remember initially talking to him about his preferred treatment methods and he said that he described them as "chaotic". Over the years Eric and I got to be very good friends. When I left the state hospital after six years, he was the one who threw my going away party at his sprawling hilltop home in the Encino Hills part of LA. He taught me so much about psychology and the human mind. I sat in on, and sometimes led, many group therapy sessions with him. He had a propensity to give away too many secrets of the profession and was severely reprimanded one time for attempting to teach some of us how to interpret Rorschach results. This happened when a fellow doctor dropped in on one of our sessions and apparently didn't like what he saw. Dr. Ellison was thought to be a little strange and unconventional by many of his colleagues and perhaps this was best illustrated by the inscription on his business card, which read: Dr. Eric Ellison, PSYCHOtheRAPIST.

And of course there were many, many others. I worked directly or indirectly with scores of professionals; some I had yet to meet and others who I never knew where they went after they left the unit. It's hard to remember exactly who was there and who was not at any given time. I think that all of us are inextricably linked to the history of the hospital. Anyone who worked there that is still alive, and I mean the people that were directly exposed to the patients being treated there, have their own memories about the experiences they encountered. I'm sure people would tell the story in many different ways, but the one underlying truth is the common and sometimes dark and disturbing experience that we all shared.

Probably the most impressionable, and sometimes intimidating, person that I worked with early on was a man who looked and acted like a character right out of a fictional book written about life in a mental hospital. He was Dr. Charles Letty. He was one of two psychiatrists on the unit when I started there. Dr. Letty was probably in his late sixties or early seventies, had white hair and wore the same slightly worn-looking black suits, white shirt and black tie every day. He sometimes used a cane to get around. He commanded respect in everything he did. When Dr. Letty phoned the nursing station and wanted something done for him it was done STAT. He was a legend around the hospital and I'm sure throughout the world of psychiatry at that time.

Usually after conducting an interview in his office, with patient and staff present, he would have the patient excused and keep the staff behind to further discuss the patient's condition and treatment plan. He would explain to us in intricate detail, often in very Freudian terms, what exactly was going on inside this person's head. One time I was sitting in with him and some others while he was seeing a psychotically depressed patient. He asked the patient several questions and then excused him. He asked us to stay afterwards. The doctor asked us all for our thoughts about this individual and we all thought that he seemed clinically depressed but perhaps he could get better with treatment and medication. He sat back in his big wooden swivel chair and said "He has already made up his mind to kill himself, it is just a matter of when and where." I don't know if he ever killed himself but I'm sure he probably did. It was all interesting and new to me and I had no reason to doubt his analogies, nor did anyone else.

Dr. Letty was the self-proclaimed inventor of the infamous drug cocktail, the #1. This was a combination of drugs that were given intramuscularly to tranquilize patients with severe psychotic symptoms. It was one of the first things I learned how to prepare, as it was used quite extensively at that time. Even though Dr. Letty apparently invented this cocktail in a syringe, the #1 and many other combinations of psychotropic drugs were being used throughout the hospital by most of the doctors. The term "Polypharmacology" was coined to describe using multiple drugs in combination with each other. There were variations of the #1 but the most common one that was prescribed, as a PRN (as needed) or STAT (immediately), was a combination of 25mg Thorazine, 5mg Stelazine and 1/150th grains of hyoscine. The hyoscine was given to counter possible side effects from the Phenothyazines (a class of antipsychotic drugs) and acted as a twilight drug. It was a very, very potent mixture and would subdue almost anyone in a matter of minutes.

Besides being known for inventing the #1, Doctor Letty was also known as a staunch believer of electro convulsive therapy, also called ECT. Millions of people worldwide were introduced to "Shock Treatments" in the famous movie "One Flew over the Cuckoo's Nest".

My first-hand knowledge of this technique and the fact that I directly participated in it many times, I guess makes me somewhat of an authority on the subject, at least from what I remember. ECT was used in state hospitals up to the end of the 1970's. The so called benefits of it were to treat severely disturbed people by sending a current of electricity directly through the lobes of the brain, essentially blocking out the thought patterns that were causing the symptoms. It was thought to be effective in treating depression, acute schizophrenia, catatonia, bipolar disorder, suicidal tendencies, and people with these conditions who were not responding to medication. The grand mal seizure that occurs as a result of the shock through the brain is what actually causes the cessation of these thoughts. It has been observed that this therapy can temporarily stop violent and aggressive behavior, active hallucinations and delusions and suicidal tendencies. It was generally seen as a "last resort" by most professionals.

I believe it was the first or second day on the job that I was summoned to assist in administering ECT to a group of patients in a large dormitory style room right next to the nursing station. It was done there so that the patients could be easily checked on following their treatment and monitored carefully until they woke up and were ready to go back to their own rooms. The room had approximately twenty beds placed in rows. A crash cart was wheeled into the room along with oxygen and I believe a heart monitor and/or an EEG monitor. I know there was a lot of equipment set up in the room but it is hard for me to remember exactly what was used, as it was such a long time ago. Everything was set up carefully before each patient was brought in for their treatment. On a tray was a tongue depressor, stethoscope, KY jelly and the anesthetic and muscle relaxer. There was also a blood pressure cuff and leather arm and leg restraints, and various other medical supplies. A separate cart with a little metal box with dials, meters and wires with electrodes on the ends was also wheeled into place by the bed. The ECT machine was plugged into the wall and the stage was set.

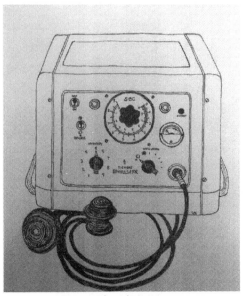

Drawing by Valerie Kamen

Depiction of ECT Machine Commonly Used at that Time

As I recall it, Dr. Letty would come out of his office at the far end of the hallway and walk down to the nursing station. He would then have a couple of techs make the rounds with him to pick the patients that would receive electroconvulsive therapy that day. This was almost always given involuntarily. Sometimes there would only be one or two and sometimes there would be up to eight or ten picked at a time. He would simply say "Him and him and him" while he pointed his finger at them. I'm sure he knew exactly which patients he would shock that day. I'm not sure if it was discussed with any of them beforehand. One patient at a time was brought into the room. They were laid down on the bed and the anesthetic and muscle relaxant given. The anesthetic was given by the doctor or a nurse intravenously. The anesthetic given was usually Methohexital and the muscle relaxant was Anectine, as far as I can remember. The monitors were attached and the blood pressure cuff put on the patient's arm.

Surprisingly most of these people, and I'm convinced it was because of the acute state of mind they were in, were really not aware what was happening to them. They usually put up little resistance. Virtually every patient on the unit was prescribed medication that was given two to three times daily. Some patients were on very high doses of anti-psychotic drugs to begin with. ECT, like I said before, was originally intended to be given only as a last resort. Over a period of time, however, it became more and more routine and was perhaps even indiscriminately used. Of course that is just my opinion. Dr. Letty and other psychiatrists that administered ECT in the sanctuary of the state hospital would argue that it was done for the betterment of the patients; and in many cases they were right. ECT was sometimes given repeatedly, over a period of time to patients to achieve the desired results.

It took only a couple of minutes for these drugs to take effect. After the patient was asleep they would be strapped into the bed for their own safety. Four of us would line up, two on each side of the bed, to hold the patient down during the convulsion. Dr. Letty would then turn on the ECT machine and make the proper adjustments. I believe it was about 1.5 volts of electricity that would directly pass through the brain. KY jelly was applied to the temples of the patient and to the electrodes at the end of the wires. The electrodes were put in place on the patient's temples and a rubber mouthpiece or taped tongue depressor was used to keep the patient from swallowing or biting off his tongue during the procedure. The muscle relaxer that is injected helps prevent broken bones, especially in the rib cage, as a result of the violent convulsion that occurs. When everyone was ready the doctor would turn the dial on the box to a desired level.

Wham! There would be an immediate convulsion of the entire body that was so intense that the first time I saw it, it made me tremble in my boots. The seizure usually lasted about a minute before subsiding, sometimes longer. The patient would buck up and down and foam at the mouth as his eyes rolled back in his head. Loud snorting noises and heavy interrupted gasps for breath were followed by the twitching of the body until it stopped. After the initial seizure was over the patient would fall back into a deep sleep. The doctor would closely monitor the patient's vital signs and heart and brain activity until he thought that they had tolerated the treatment well enough. We then rolled the patient onto his side to promote breathing and adjusted him in the bed. The leather restraints would be removed and the bed pushed next to the wall or the one preceding it so that the patient couldn't roll off and hurt himself.

The next patient would then be brought in and the procedure was repeated and so on until they had all been convulsed. It took about two hours before the patients woke up, confused, and staggered back to their beds, usually with our help. They didn't talk, they didn't act out, and they didn't do anything except go to their room. It was usually later that day that they would emerge, not remembering anything about what had happened. Their minds seemed to be mostly blank. I cannot remember one incident where a patient's life was endangered, as this was taken very seriously and every medical precaution necessary was used.

Before I left the state hospital the laws were already changing regarding ECT. The seemingly barbaric style in which patients were given these treatments, almost like cattle, came to a halt. The only way shock treatments could be given was with the mutual consent of three doctors and later, for a period of time, only with the added signature of the governor of California. By 1979 it was stopped completely. This therapy is still used today in private hospital settings throughout the United States, but is highly constrained by state and local laws. Sometimes the results are dramatic and very successful. ECT has been known to actually halt severe symptoms in some people but I think you would have to use the word "Cure" loosely.

So if you saw the movie, One Flew over the Cuckoo's Nest, the scene where they give Jack Nicholson electroconvulsive therapy is fairly realistic. They kind of minimize the actual process but the audience gets an idea of how it works. When I went to see the 1975 movie I had already assisted in giving ECT many times and chuckled to myself when the audience gasped. You had to have been there to get the full experience of how dramatic it really was. I never really talked to many people outside the hospital about this and other experiences I had there. It was just something that I kept to myself.

Photograph by Robert Inglis
The Iconic Bell Tower

CHAPTER 3
A Strange Mixture Indeed

We live in a world of tremendous diversity among its inhabitants. No two people are alike. Identical twins may look almost exactly the same on the outside but they can think and act differently than their doppelganger counterpart. As we walk around this remarkable planet we call home we encounter hundreds of thousands of people in the course of our lifetimes. We initially perceive people based on their outward appearance and behavior. When you meet a person for the first time you automatically size them up, so to speak. If someone greets you enthusiastically with a big smile on their face you probably would be more inclined to interact with that person rather than a person who won't make eye contact and seems more withdrawn. Human interactions are very complicated as we know, but there seems to be an invisible line that shouldn't be crossed. On the other side of that line are the people that this story is about.

I'm sure you have run across people in a public place or while walking down the street that strike you as being different or strange or even scary. They stand out in the crowd. You can tell that they don't conform to the normal standards of society that we use to judge people.

You might think to yourself or tell the other people you are with "Look at that weirdo" or "What's wrong with him?" The person may be agitated and acting bizarrely. They may be talking to themselves or shouting obscenities. They may be severely disheveled. They may seem to not even notice that you or anyone else is near them. You kind of think to yourself "How did she get that way?" or "Who takes care of him?" or "Where do they get food?" Existentially it is difficult to justify this in your mind so you walk on by, never knowing what happened to that person, how they survived.

Photographs by Robert Inglis

The hospital could be a dark and gloomy place at times.

The hospital, as I said, was divided into two main sections - the mentally ill on one side and the developmentally disabled or "retarded" on the other. Note that I am not using the word "retarded" in any sort of derogatory manner; just that in the 1970's the general public probably was more familiar with that term than with the term "developmentally disabled". There were the other outlying divisions that housed the children, the aged, and the alcoholics. You might say that the most talked about and the most written about group of people that inhabited the state hospitals then were the mentally ill, the psychotic and neurotic personalities that bewildered our senses with their strange exotic behavior. The fact that there are severely retarded people who are completely incapable of taking care of themselves without being housed in an institution is sad but true. There are many millions of people with slight or moderate mental deficiencies who are able to live decent lives and make a real contribution to society, holding down jobs and even having their own families. Many of these individuals are loved and give love in return. The professional people who work day in and day out with higher functioning retarded citizens, people with Down's syndrome, deserve much praise in my opinion. They can really make a difference in a person's life. The halfway homes and outlying day treatment facilities that are scattered throughout the country serve a great purpose. Unfortunately there are those whose intelligence is so low that an institution or hospital setting is the only place where they can be taken care of.

Camarillo State Hospital required that all residents be ambulatory, whether or not they were mentally ill or developmentally disabled. Some of the other state hospitals in California did, and still do as far as I know, house non-ambulatory developmentally disabled patients. I once visited Agnews State hospital near San Jose and saw firsthand a number of these special needs people. Most of them did not have a measurable IQ and required 24 hour nursing. I saw individuals that never developed in the womb and resembled "Monsters". I saw hydrocephalic patients with fifty plus inch heads and tiny little bodies that could only lay in a crib and be tube fed. I saw the freaks of nature that almost no one ever gets to see unless you worked there. I talked to a technician while I was there and she told me a story about when a voter's rights group came knocking on the door basically demanding that they be allowed to sign these patients up to vote. They said "Fine, come on in." After entering the unit and taking a quick look around the people quickly apologized and left as fast as they could.

The ambulatory DD's at Camarillo were by no means high functioning. Most of them could crudely feed themselves but almost all of them needed a lot of help with bathing, grooming and dressing. Very few could talk or had a rudimentary vocabulary at best. My first experience with them was during training in the psych tech program. We were split into small groups and assigned to various units to observe and assist the staff. This was for a period of several weeks as I recall. There were female units and male units. I was fortunate enough, or unfortunate enough, depending how you looked at it, to have been assigned to both male and female units.

The way the units were designed throughout the hospital was with the patients' rooms or dorms situated along either side of long hallways with a centralized large dayroom.

The dayroom was where most of the patients stayed during the day. On the M.I. side the patients could watch TV, play cards, smoke cigarettes, etc. On the D.D. side the day rooms may have had a TV but it was mainly for the benefit of the employees. The dayroom was used to keep the patients in a single location so that they could be more easily watched and cared for. The day we arrived on one of these male D.D. units there were probably six or seven of us, both male and female students. The first sounds we heard when the door was opened were grunting and screaming noises and loud repetitive shouting resonating throughout the unit.

Upon entering the dayroom there were approximately twenty or thirty male patients and a handful of staff members frantically running around trying to keep control of what looked like a very stressful situation. Some of the patients were banging their heads on the hard walls, one was completely naked and furiously masturbating on the floor and others were just rocking back and forth continuously while moaning and drooling down their chins. Many had protective helmets on to minimize serious head injuries. Several patients began to approach us with outstretched arms almost as if they wanted to engulf us as a zombie would in the movies. The technicians grabbed them and forcefully moved them out of the way. On one side of the dayroom there were three or four large doughnut like objects that had people placed inside of them. They were heavy duty, stuffed vinyl protective devices designed to keep the worst of the worst from attacking other patients or doing harm to themselves. During the course of that day we learned that if these people were not put in the doughnuts they potentially could do unspeakable things. We were told that some were capable of eating the nose and ears off of other patients and that they had even been known to swallow entire sheets and pillow cases or attempt to devour a chair or sofa. Needless to say that when I previously mentioned that a lot of the students dropped out in the early stages of training, this was one of those times.

During the course of my employment I did my share of overtime, as most of us did. There was such a high rate of people calling in sick that overtime was easily obtainable. I didn't work nearly as much overtime as my co-worker Gill Smith and others, but I usually managed to get in four or five shifts a month. It helped pay the bills. It got so bad at times that the program office would actually send two people to your house to make sure you were there and that you were indeed sick. The state was constantly on a budget and hated paying out all of the expensive overtime checks. They made no bones about it. Even with that the problem persisted until the day I left.

I did overtime on my unit as well as many other units all over the hospital. I became familiar with a lot of these units and knew what to expect when I turned the key. Some of the many units I speak of were the female D.D. units. I soon found out why but these units had the reputation of being the most dangerous and crazy units you could step foot into. I remember being literally afraid for my life on a couple of occasions. You had to be wide awake and alert at all times. Never turn your back on some of these individuals.

The one incident that really stands out in my mind was when I was walking into the dayroom and was approaching one of the female staff members, who was sitting in a chair keeping an eye on the mayhem, when out of the blue one of the most aggressive patients, a young, wiry female with an IQ of about thirty, ran up in back of her and slammed her and the chair to the ground. Her head cracked on the floor. Several of us rushed to her assistance and she was subsequently taken away in an ambulance. The technician was severely injured as a result and I'm not sure if she ever came back to work. I was lucky to have never been hurt seriously while working on the D.D. units, male or female.

Not all of these patients were aggressive to the point where they were a danger to others. A good portion of them simply could not care for themselves. Groups of these women would be "herded" into the shower room where they were forced to use soap to clean their private areas and then basically sprayed down like cattle. It was the only way to get them clean. Then the ordeal of getting them dressed, brushing their hair and getting them to the dining room was always a major chore as it tended to wear one's patience very thin. At the end of an eight hour shift everyone was exhausted.

Believe it or not there was a small population of D.D.s who actually were allowed to spend time outside in the fenced-in courtyards. There was one of these special people who was kind of a legend around the hospital. His name was Francis. He had microcephaly, which is a condition where the skull does not grow to its normal size, therefore not allowing the brain to develop normally. People with microcephalus have very tiny heads and look very strange to see in person. They have been cast in old Hollywood freak movies and used in carnival side shows. Francis had an unusually small cranium, even by these standards. He would be let out into a secure area during the day and would stand in the exact same spot, peering out, with his hands tightly clinched to the chain link fence. He couldn't talk but almost seemed to have a way of communicating with passersby, who would talk to him and always get a kick out of his coy little smile. He would make little mewling-like noises but avoided all eye contact. We always talked about "Francis the micro". He had been there most of his life. I wonder what might have happened to him when they closed down the hospital. Hopefully he was transferred to another hospital or facility that would take care of this gentle soul.

My experiences working with the children in Camarillo State Hospital were not as extensive as with some of the other populations but I will never forget them. During my training I spent several weeks on one of the children's units learning as much as I could about learning deficiencies, behavioral problems, hyperactivity and especially autism. These children had varying degrees of illness. Some of them were almost impossible to manage because of their unpredictability and hyperactive nature. I was so drawn in trying to understand how their minds worked, what they thought and how they saw the world around them. It seemed like some of them were just unreachable, like there was no one in there. Severely autistic children sometimes never can be reached.

I noticed that autistic children often exhibit rocking movements similar to that of a retarded person, but they are not retarded. The self-stimming rituals they do with their hands, holding their hands in front of their face and twiddling their fingers, is a classic behavior that often time follows them into adulthood. We used to pose and answer the question "What happens to autistic children? They become adult schizophrenics". I have always been fascinated by these special children and adolescents. I came out of my six plus year career at the hospital relatively unscathed with the exception of one scar on my left wrist. I was standing in a hallway on the unit when one of the more hyperactive autistic children ran at me full speed. I held my arms up in front of me in a protective stance but he managed to inflict a fairly deep cut on my arm as he flew by me. Sometimes when people gather around to compare scars, I am usually the only one that can say that I have a scar from an autistic child.

The hospital had a research program that was fairly well funded while I worked there. I remember during tech school watching a short documentary, produced by the hospital's research unit, which was about one of the autistic children. Her name was Pamela. They spent a lot of money and had some of the best doctors and researchers working with her over a period of several years. She was a young child with severe autism that was one of those "unreachable" cases. During the course of the film you can see how they used many different conditioning techniques and immersed her in state-of-the-art approaches in an attempt to draw her out of her shell and into our reality. The results were startling. She made tremendous progress and the film and her story made national news at the time. She was by no means cured or even acted like what we would call normal, but compared to the way she was, it was remarkable. She could bathe herself, dress herself, had a simple vocabulary and seemed as though she understood where she was and what was going on around her. Sadly, that old saying "All good things must come to an end", came to be true with Pamela. Either the funding ran out or the program dissolved or something of that nature ended the research on Pamela and other people. It was very disheartening for me to come to work one day to see that she had been admitted to Unit 77 as an adult schizophrenic and later transferred to a long term chronic unit. Any demonstrable evidence of her previous achievements were gone. She had completely regressed and was once again incapable of taking care of herself, requiring the shelter of an institution.

I also gained experience working with adolescents, geriatrics, alcoholics and other groups of patients both during the tech training program and while employed at the hospital. However the largest group, and perhaps the most interesting and the most talked about, were the adult mentally ill. This group of people are the ones that conjure up the mythical and sordid history that people think about when you say "Mental institution" or "Insane asylum". Countless books and movies have attempted to capture this taboo subject into words and film. The incredible variety of mentally ill patients, with every conceivable diagnosis and condition, walked the halls of Camarillo State hospital for many decades. I personally saw thousands of these cases during my time there.

My unit, as I stated earlier, was a short term program designed to deal with patients with acute onset problems and chronic conditions and to treat them according to their diagnosis or behavior and make the determination as to whether they would be discharged, transferred to a longer term unit or stay voluntarily for a period of time. They ranged from being homeless drifters to highly successful business people, as mental illness does not choose sides. The longest anyone stayed on my unit was about a month, sometimes a little longer. All of this was done in accordance with the laws of the State of California. I'll get into legal aspects of patient care a little later on in the story. Since we were an admissions type program, and given the nature of the law, there was a definite "revolving door" aspect that we grew to expect. Sometimes we would see the same person admitted several times a year.

We treated people with varying degrees of neurosis, OCD, ADD, adult autism, depression, drug addiction, behavior problems, alcoholism, drug induced psychosis, schizoaffective disorder, manic depressive illness (or Bi-Polar as it is called now), mania, epilepsy, mental retardation and even those with severe physical disabilities or neurological diseases, such as Huntington's chorea or Parkinson's disease. But schizophrenia was probably the most serious and debilitating mental illness that we saw, and probably the most difficult to treat effectively. A person suffering from schizophrenia can be extremely withdrawn at one end of the spectrum to being uncontrollably violent at the other end. They can hallucinate, they can hear voices in their head and they are generally split from the reality that we know, not being able to understand what is real and what is not.

Although there are many types or subtypes of schizophrenia described in psychiatric literature the most common forms, and the ones that we were generally the most exposed to, are the paranoid type, the catatonic type, the psychotically depressed type and the chronic undifferentiated type. There were rows of buildings in the bowels of the hospital that housed hundreds of patients with chronic schizophrenia. We simply called them "Chronics" or the "Chronic Units". These were long term units that had patients that literally had been there for most of their adult lives. Schizophrenia usually appears as an early adult onset. Children are not usually described as schizophrenic but autism can lead to adult schizophrenia. It is easier to describe these mental illnesses in a textbook format.

Paranoid Schizophrenia is characterized by delusional thoughts, holding firmly to beliefs that are not true, that you have incredible powers, are famous, and that people are out to get you. Paranoid schizophrenics may also suffer from auditory or visual hallucinations.

Catatonic Schizophrenia is a form of withdrawal which is marked by the patient literally "freezing up". They may become immobile for long periods of time and may develop a waxy flexibility, where you can actually bend and mold their extremities like a clay figure. The first time I saw this I took hold of the man's arm and pulled it straight up, out of curiosity. It stayed where I let go. I then bent his head to the side and it stayed bent. He did not move from that position until I changed him back. This is very strange to see. Waxy flexibility can usually be controlled with a tranquilizer regiment.

Psychotic depression is marked by prolonged periods of depression and immobility where the person may also be experiencing auditory hallucinations and having intense feelings of despair, worthlessness and helplessness. The person becomes withdrawn and depressed to the point where there is no escape from it and can be predictably suicidal. Psychotic depression is a subtype of major depressive disorder or simply "depression". The two may have crossover symptoms but psychotic depression is usually more severe because of its psychotic features. I have noticed that individuals suffering from this type of depression may take on a deeply drawn look and that their skin color may also change or darken, with an ashen appearance, while in a deep depression.

And finally there is the chronic undifferentiated type which is a kind of catch all diagnosis that is given to people that may exhibit several classic symptoms of schizophrenia. These symptoms may include withdrawal, depression, agitation, hallucinations and abnormal thinking and bizarre behavior. These patients may also exhibit bizarre posturing and speak in a meaningless word salad. It is characterized by long periods of illness without remission.

And as I said there are other subtypes of schizophrenia, such as catastrophic schizophrenia and schizoaffective disorder, which is a hybrid condition combining schizophrenia and bipolar disorder and depression. Schizoaffective disorder, because it is so complicated, may be harder to diagnose or pinpoint. People with this disorder often hold down a job and appear to lead a normal life to some, but can fall victim to these symptoms and may experience full psychotic breaks.

So getting back to when I started and in the early weeks of my employment, I can remember some of the patients that really made an impression on me. One of them was a young guy, in his twenties, who was admitted with what seemed to be a true drug induced psychosis. He had no previous mental health issues prior to then. I made it a point to talk to him as much as I could. I really wanted to get inside his head for some reason. We spent a lot of time in the recreation room at the end of the hallway, where there was a ping pong table and an old beat up piano. This was right in the middle of the early seventies rock explosion and he had an affinity for David Bowie. He would play Suffragette City over and over on that old piano. He was obviously a decent musician with a good singing voice. In between these marathon piano banging sessions we would sit and talk about his problems.

He was of course given major tranquilizing drugs, as was almost everyone with psychotic symptoms. It wasn't until several days after being admitted for acute paranoid symptoms that he was able to calm down enough, with the aid of the medication, to talk about and describe in detail his hallucinations and delusions. He described to me the horrors that had gripped his mind after taking LSD only a couple of times. He swore to me that he not only saw the devil himself but that he had talked to him. He described the devil standing right in front of him stirring a big boiling pot of bubbling liquid with flames shooting out of it. The devil had horns and a tail just like you would see in a cartoon or a horror movie. He said it scared him so much he started screaming at the top of his lungs and running around in a panic. He could not escape it. The result was his hospitalization.

He had one or two flashbacks while on the unit, but after a couple of weeks he was discharged by the doctor, apparently free of any psychotic symptoms. He was never admitted to our unit again, but he may have been admitted to another unit. I hope not. Sometimes mind altering drugs like LSD can cause temporary psychosis and the person recovers fully and sometimes it triggers something in that person that follows them throughout their lives.

Another strange case of paranoia involved a man who was brought to us with the belief that he was being followed by the CIA and that he was in grave danger. I know this sounds cliché but there it was, a textbook case right before our eyes. From the minute he was admitted to our unit he was in a state of constant terror, running to each window and looking out saying "They're out there, they're out there"! He would go to each of us and ask us if we had seen anyone that was trying to get to him. Ron would say "No, I think you are imagining these people". Jean Winters would say "No I haven't seen anyone". Dr. Ellison would try to convince him that it was all in his head, but he wasn't buying it. This went on for several days and it got worse before it got better. He had picked up some small rocks somewhere that he had in his possession and claimed that they were genuine moon rocks and that they were of such great value that these people, the CIA and other dark organizations, were willing to kill him in order to get them. The shear amount of stress that this poor man must have endured during this episode, and the amount of energy he used to fight it in his head, had to have taken a heavy toll on him not only mentally but physically as well. At times he looked completely exhausted as if he so desperately wanted to escape his terror but just could not relax for one minute, knowing, in his mind, that he was not safe and that things were not ok, that he could trust no one. He would say things like "You don't understand." or "How can I make you realize that these people are out there right now." or "These rocks are more valuable than you can possibly imagine."

After about a week, and as the anti-psychotic medication started to take effect, he slowly began to relax. I came to work one morning to see him talking to some of the other nursing staff in a calm, rational voice. He said he realized now that he was imagining the whole thing. He hugged us all and began crying. He handed me the "moon rocks" and I disposed of them. He was discharged soon afterward with follow up care and a running prescription for the tranquilizers that he so desperately needed. This time we made a difference.

To describe the way some of the more severe cases really were is difficult to put down in words. You almost had to have been there and seen them to believe that there were actually real people like this. The chronic schizophrenics generally were very withdrawn. They would spend their day sitting in the dayroom, smoking cigarettes, drinking coffee, talking to themselves, rocking back and forth, self-stimming and occasionally acting out. They were generally fairly easy to manage but it was usually hard to get them to participate in anything. The psychosis that many of them suffered from was often too severe, as they were lost somewhere else, trapped in their own minds. Surprisingly most of them had good appetites as food and cigarettes seemed to be their only priorities. You could tell if someone was a chronic schizophrenic not only by the way they behaved but by looking at their fingers. They all chain smoked and would smoke a cigarette all the way down to the filter and beyond. Their fingers were so stained by the tar in the tobacco that it would be very, very difficult to remove. We didn't even try. Their hygiene was generally very poor and a lot of them had missing teeth or no teeth at all. Those who had slipped into a deep catatonic state were harder to care for and sometimes required force feeding and bathing until they came out of it.

We also had to treat very violent and acutely disturbed people who were unpredictable and considered a danger to others. These people could be very scary to deal with. We not only had to formulate some sort of treatment plan for them, and implement it, but at the same time we had to make sure that they did not harm us or the other patients. To achieve this, and to remain safe, we had to use selected treatment methods that were at our disposal. Besides drug therapy, such as the #1 cocktail I described earlier, cuff and belt restraints and quiet rooms were used frequently. I'll describe in more detail the dangers that we encountered with these wild individuals in another chapter.

Some of the patients were allowed ground privileges. This was a privilege that must be ordered by the doctor after the patient could demonstrate that he or she was trustworthy and cognizant enough to walk around the hospital grounds or attend activities on their own. Mostly patients with ground privileges would walk to the canteen to buy candy, coffee or cigarettes. Some just wanted to get fresh air and not feel so confined. If a patient broke the rules or caused trouble while out on ground privileges, they would usually be confined back on the unit. There were occasions when a patient would have an episode while outside of the unit and the hospital police would be called to handle the situation. There were even times when a patient would either decide to walk off of the hospital grounds or attempt to escape. I remember one incident where we had to spend hours pulling the cactus needles out of a patient's skin who was returned by the hospital police after he had made the very poor decision to escape by way of the steep mountains that surrounded the hospital. The local mountains in that area are filled with thousands of prickly pear cactus that are very painful if you get tangled up with them.

Unit 77 doorway from courtyard to dayroom

I only saw one patient the entire time I worked at Camarillo State Hospital that had been given a prefrontal lobotomy. This is a surgical procedure that was once used commonly in the dark history of treating mental illness, but is rarely used now. It is a brain surgery to relieve or eliminate severe mental or behavioral problems in someone. The nerve tract to the frontal lobe of the brain is severed, leaving the patient with a marked change in their personality and ability to perceive things. The particular patient that I saw was only on our unit for a couple of days. I believe he was transferred to another state hospital, maybe Atascadero. There wasn't much left of his mind. He looked and acted like a zombie or a

Frankenstein monster. There was no interaction, no emotion, no nothing. It was considered after time to be a cruel, inhumane procedure and was generally abolished. Insulin shock therapy and then electro convulsive therapy was the more accepted alternative.

We received an incredibly large man as a transfer from Atascadero State Hospital one time who was the embodiment of the boogie man. The history in his chart revealed that he had murdered his entire family and was declared insane during the trial. He stood about six feet ten inches tall and probably weighed four hundred plus pounds, with flaming red hair and freckles. He was dressed in orange overalls and white tennis shoes. He walked around slowly, breathing heavily and just seemed to be staring into space. He didn't talk but when he made eye contact with you it felt like he was looking into your soul. It was really creepy. I can't recall why he was released from Atascadero and transferred to us, but he didn't stay long. The really incredible thing about this case was that he was on a maintenance dose of 800 mg of Mellaril, which is a heavy tranquilizer, twice a day, or BID as we would say. He also had a standing PRN (as needed) of a really high dose of tranquilizers that could be given if he got out of control. Now the thing that makes this so incredible is that the average dose for a human is perhaps 25mg once or twice a day! We could not believe that this man could withstand this dose and live. Before we gave it to him initially we made sure that it was not a mistake. We were all so relieved when he was discharged from our unit and that he didn't become out of control. It would had taken many people to subdue this giant, scary beast.

As many activities as possible were planned for this always changing group of people. As you can tell there were many who simply could not or would not participate in any group functions. For those patients who were willing and able, certain things were provided. There was the recreation room with the ping pong table and piano, where we also held group therapy sessions, and there was the arts and crafts room at the other end of the hallway where Bob Rodriguez would have Monday through Friday painting, sculpting and other craft activities planned. Each unit had an attached courtyard where some of the patients could go during the day to be outside and to get exercise. Sometimes the kitchen would provide us with everything we needed for a good old fashioned barbeque of hot dogs and hamburgers and all the trimmings. The patients loved that. The courtyard also had a volleyball court, a basketball goal, a punching bag, as well as benches to sit on. Dr. Ellison would organize a volleyball game almost every day. The patients that were able to play were encouraged to get involved and it turned out to be a great way to blow off steam for them as well as the staff. It was almost impossible for anyone to escape from the high walls of the courtyard, in case someone bolted out of the door, but they occasionally did. On rare occasions, if we felt it was safe enough, we would leave the door to the courtyard open and let the patients roam about freely.

One time a very violent patient, a large muscular African-American man with drug induced paranoia, did bolt out of the door and into the courtyard. We tried to coax him back in but he was too agitated and we felt that he was capable of harming people at that point. We called the hospital police and they arrived in force. That was the only time in my life that I got hit with mace. One of the officers managed to spray him directly in his eyes with a large amount of mace and some of it got in my eyes after a bunch of us tackled him to the ground. It was very painful and irritating for me but I can only imagine what the patient went through.

Photograph by Robert Inglis
Entrance to an Old Courtyard

Patients would be taken to the pool to swim when the weather was warm enough and every Sunday two of us would escort some of the patients to church. We would also take groups to the Movie Theater and bowling alley. Sometimes we would gather up several patients and simply go on a walk around the hospital grounds. All extracurricular activities were thought of as good therapy for those patients who were well enough to participate.

So you kind of get an idea of the incredible variety of the patient population and what we were up against. It was indeed a strange mixture of humanity. There is probably no place on earth where you can see so many different mental afflictions in one place than in the confines of an institution such as Camarillo State Hospital. Some scary, some docile, some curable, most not curable. I remember seeing a list of the 100 most dangerous occupations in the State of California at the time I worked there and psychiatric nursing was nearly at the top, alongside peace officers.

CHAPTER 4
Life, Work, Fun

Somewhere intertwined in all the craziness and madness that was now my new life at the hospital was my other life, that of a young man who was just feeling his way through his early twenties with all of the trials and tribulations that go with that. The eye-opening things that I had been subjected to so far definitely were changing the way I viewed the world. I had always thought that I was capable of profound thinking but the absurd profundity of life was now staring me in the face. I decided to try to separate my professional life from my private life. Easier said than done because your professional life becomes your private life as well at that point.

I grew up with my share of casual friends. I, like many people, had a very close knit group of friends who were the people that I always associated with. I was never an extremely social person, but I got along with people and I certainly didn't have many enemies. My new coworkers at the hospital were by association my newest set of friends. I can't say that any of them became really close friends during the entire time I worked at Camarillo, but we did manage to get together sometimes and blow off a little steam.

In 1975 I went to a party at a friend of mine's house and met a young 18 year old girl, who was a friend of a friend of a friend. We hit it off immediately and began seeing each other as much as possible. I had just purchased a brand new Ford mini truck and was planning to go on a cross country driving trip with my older brother. Well, I went on the 7000 mile driving trip with my brother and as soon as I got back Nora and I decided to get married. Looking back on it, it was really foolish, but young love or infatuation or whatever you want to call it can be very powerful. Our marriage only lasted five years and was filled with good times and bad times. We got married in Las Vegas and moved into an apartment at first and then to that tiny little duplex on the beach. Needless to say I picked up yet another set of friends, hers, and a new set of relatives.

I was enjoying life at that point. I was a real grown up! I had a good paying job with great benefits, a new truck, a funky little beach pad and I was married. I took the state board exam in Los Angeles and passed on the first try. I was now a fully licensed psychiatric technician. After a few months on the evening shift I put in a request to work the day shift. To my amazement I got the transfer. It worked out very nicely for me because I now had the opportunity to get a taste of the action on the day shift and I was able to spend more time with Nora, as she also worked during the day.

I always seemed to have plenty of time off from work. The way the State Hospital scheduled employee days off was interesting. Everyone rotated forward one day every week to where you would have two three day weekends in a row. So for instance you would start with Monday and Tuesday off and then the next week you would have Tuesday and Wednesday off and so on until you got to Friday, Saturday and Sunday, then Saturday, Sunday and Monday, and then back to Monday and Tuesday. Everyone seemed to love this schedule. The one bummer was that we only got paid once a month, but that taught us how to budget and spend wisely (ha ha).

We threw a lot of parties at the beach. Half the time I didn't even know many of the people in my own house. Some people would hear the music blasting and just walk in off the street. I had four huge Harman Kardon speakers and a 150 watt per channel receiver that put out incredible sound. There was a true laid back beach attitude in those days. Nobody cared how loud the music was or how late people's parties went into the night. The beer was always flowing and the barbeque was always lit. It still amazes me how I was able to make it to work on time the next day after those crazy parties. But like I said, after the unit supervisor laid the law on me, I was never late again. I just sucked it up and didn't complain. You can only blame yourself right?

Even though I was probably abusing my body with all of the beer drinking and parties, I managed to stay in very good physical condition. I had always been athletic from an early age and was not overweight. In fact I was lean and muscular. In between my social life and work I played a lot of basketball and did a considerable amount of hiking. I took up tennis in my early twenties as well and got pretty good at it.

The disco wave started in 1975 but I never got caught up in it. I was raised on blues, folk music and rock and roll. My buddies and I, and sometimes my wife, would all cram into someone's van or mini truck with a camper shell and sojourn to as many concerts in LA and Santa Barbara as we could. I never smoked much pot but most of my friends did. When we would arrive at the concerts and pile out in the parking lot the marijuana smoke would pour out of the vehicle as if it were on fire. Wow, those were the days. Somehow, despite the wild nature of me and my friends and all of the escapades that I remember, I was still able to maintain a professional attitude and appearance at work. I guess I took my job seriously.

As I said I got to know some of the people I worked with well enough to associate with them off duty. Amy Harris, one of the RN's who worked on my unit, used to have some incredible parties at her big house in Oxnard. She knew a lot of people at the hospital and her parties were a mixture of hospital workers, technicians, RN's, social workers and doctors. I met people from all over the hospital at those parties. It was at one of those parties where I saw people dancing to disco music for the first time. It was funny to see the some of the people dressed in their disco clothing, with the gold chains and long side burns and bell bottoms and the women with their corresponding flashy outfits, and some of us dressed in blue jeans, boots and shoulder length hair. Looking back at the mid-seventies there was really a striking contrast between styles and attitudes.

The hospital was a big place and there were a lot of employees. It is no misconception that we had our share of "weirdos" working there. The night shifts all over the hospital had a small percentage of marginal staff members. I heard it said more than once that "the employees are as crazy as the patients!" While I was working for the county in-patient facility I saw at least two, present or former Camarillo staffers who I recognized, admitted for treatment. I'm not sure if some of these people had just been there a long time and were kind of "grandfathered in" or if the hospital's hiring and screening standards were not up to par. At the time of my hiring I thought that everything was done professionally and thoroughly.

There was an older technician that I worked with early on in my employment. He would always tell me about his aspirations to run for the mayor of Oxnard. He would ramble on about how he thought the government was screwed up and that people should take on more civic responsibility. He said he had a plan to make Oxnard run like a spinning top if he was elected. I totally encouraged him and admired him for his interest in city politics. I began to notice that he was very underweight and that he would sometimes seem very shaky. I didn't give it much thought after that. We became friends and shared a lot about one another. One day he confided in me that he was a severe alcoholic. Over a period of time he described his drinking bouts in minute detail to me. He told me how he would drink a quart of salad oil before starting one of his binges. He said that on more than one occasion he would buy a round trip ticket to London Heathrow airport. He would drink all the way there, spend 24 hours in the bar at the airport, drinking heavily, and then drink all the way back to California! He didn't last long on our unit and I never knew what happened with him.

In order to escape the rigors of hospital life we found ways to entertain ourselves. There were a couple of local watering holes where a lot of the state employees would hang out after work. I used to drink beer and shoot pool at the Buckhorn with some of the people from the unit. This was the place where all the gossip from around the hospital would be talked about and was also the place where people could complain about their bosses and all of the needless piles of bureaucratic paper work that were bestowed on us by the desk jockeys in Sacramento. It was also a place where single people, and I assume some married people, would go to hook up. And no, I never did that; I was a good boy.

The employee homes, which were a group of dormitory style stucco buildings very near the hospital grounds, were where many, mostly single, employees lived. The rooms were plain and sparsely furnished with those old radiator heaters to keep you halfway warm. There were always parties going on day and night in the homes. I knew quite a few people who lived in the homes. I met some really cool people at those parties and listened to a lot of great music. It was kind of a throwback to the hippie days, complete with community bongs and rooms decorated with beads and Indian rugs and the like. In those days there were a lot of psychedelics floating around, which made for some interesting encounters with people. Those who lived there did so mostly out of necessity, as it was dirt cheap. They would simply take the monthly rent out of your paycheck. I think it was around seventy-five bucks a month or so. The rooms, as I said, were very small and plain but they were a place to crash and served the purpose. There was also a set of nicer homes near there that were occupied by the upper echelon of the hospital staff, such as program directors and hospital administrators.

Once in a while we did some really crazy stuff. One day several of us on the day shift somehow got into a conversation about adult movies, as they were one of the up and coming things, especially with the Deep Throat phenomenon going around. Most of us had either seen one or two porn movies or none at all. So on a bet we decided to all go together to the Pussycat Theater to see Misty Beethoven, one of the current running productions that was supposedly better than the average porno movie. Six or eight of us, including one of the social workers, all piled into a big van and went to the theater at night. We were all kind of embarrassed and two of the female employees laughed the whole way through the movie. That was the first and last trip to the adult movie theater for our crew, but it was fun.

It was not always fun and games for some of our steadfast employees, however. There were people who had serious problems in their personal lives. We all banded together, it seemed like, to come to the aid of anyone who was having bad personal problems. The most striking example of this was when we all rallied around one of our doctors, Dr. Alvin Swiner. He was one of the two medical doctors on the unit. He was not a board certified psychiatrist but rather an MD with extensive emergency room experience who managed to land a job at the state hospital despite a history of alcoholism and drinking bouts. When he first came to work on the unit he seemed fine. One day two men in black suits rang the bell. I opened the door and asked them who they were there to visit. They said they were from the IRS and were there to see Dr. Swiner. They looked like all business, no smiles.

After they left Dr. Swiner reluctantly told some of us that he owed the IRS over a million dollars in back taxes and that the IRS had basically come there to give him an ultimatum. You could tell that the doctor was very shaken up. The IRS came again the next week and the week after that. It was really taking a toll on Dr. Swiner. He had not been drinking since he started working on our unit. He really wanted to get sober and stay sober. We all liked him a great deal and he trusted in us.

One morning Dr. Swiner arrived at work drunk out of his mind. How he drove to work was a mystery to say the least. The whole thing was just too much for him. Apparently he had started drinking the night before. His wife couldn't stop him from getting in the car and called the unit shortly after he had gotten there. She was very worried about him but we assured her that we would make sure he was safe and in good hands. Jean ran up to the office from the medication room and said "You have to come and see this!" I walked down to the med room and there was Dr. Swiner sitting in a chair and being held up by Mary Baldwin so that he wouldn't fall flat on his face. He looked like holy hell. He was slurring his loud incoherent speech and drooling all over himself.

It wasn't very long after I began working on Unit 77 that I found out that if an employee came to work with a bad hangover there was a self-prescribed method used by the staff to get that employee up to speed and feeling better. Usually it was a shot of vitamin B12 in the arm, a glass of orange juice and a few hits of pure oxygen. Sometimes you could pop a valium, as the control on tranquilizers and pain killers was fairly lax and wasn't nearly as enforced as it is now. This usually snapped people out of their hangover quickly. I don't mean to say that we all did this, only every once in a while and only when it was warranted.

We had to wait quite a while for the alcohol to pass through Dr. Swiner's system and then he was given IM Valium, along with the B12 and the oxygen and orange juice. We moved him to his office and laid him down on the couch so he could sleep it off. Over the course of the next few weeks this happened several times and each time we dealt with it. Eventually his IRS problems subsided and he was able to stop drinking again. He was very grateful to us all for our support. He was a good man and a great physician with some problems. We all have them.

We stuck up for each other but when the 1976 investigation by Ventura County District Attorney Michael Bradbury into negligent deaths and abuses of patients at Camarillo State Hospital began, it shook some people to the very core.

CHAPTER 5

The Law

The laws that govern and protect those people with mental and developmental disabilities in the State of California were the bible that we all had to follow. The Lanterman-Petris-Short Act, bipartisan legislation written by these three California politicians, was signed into law by Governor Reagan in 1967 and became fully implemented in 1972, the year before I began working at Camarillo State Hospital. I became very familiar with the applicable part of it very quickly on. It was especially poignant working on an admissions unit rather than on a long term chronic unit, where the legal disposition of most of those patients had long been determined. Everything revolved around these laws; the length of stay, the treatment plan, the follow up and even the ultimate destiny of thousands of people. Everyone may have had their own opinions about a certain individual, but it was now the police officer, doctor or judge that called all the shots.

On many hundreds of occasions I saw people literally dragged onto the unit, sometimes in cuffs and belts, screaming and kicking all the way. Others put up little or no resistance. Many were disoriented, actively hallucinating and out of touch with reality. A certain percentage did have the cognition to understand where they were and what was happening to them. Regardless of their mental state at the time of admission an overwhelming number of them were there against their will.

Before 1967, in the State of California, people with severe mental problems had few rights. They were often locked up in institutions for indefinite periods of time without legal representation. This included people with developmental disabilities and chronic alcoholics. The Lanterman-Petris-Short Act set a precedent for modern mental health commitment procedures in the United States. The law not only set the guidelines for commitment, but also for safeguarding the public and providing treatment and follow up services for people with mental disabilities. It was really a landmark legislative victory for patients' rights advocates and groups like the ACLU.

The law itself was fairly complicated, with many provisions, but the premise was fairly simple. It basically said that an individual could be legally detained against their will if they were a danger to themselves, a danger to others or were gravely disabled. This was determined by a police officer or a doctor or qualified mental health authority or a judge. The person could be held up to 14 days and then placed on a temporary conservatorship after that if it was deemed necessary. A temporary conservatorship was a period of 180 days and a full conservatorship was for a period of a year at a time.

After the temporary conservatorship a full conservatorship could be granted. Conservatorship cases, just like with the general public, were done in a court setting before a judge. The conservator was a person appointed by the court who could demonstrate that they were capable of taking care of the person, including making sure that they had proper housing, food, clothing, etc. and also were able to control their bank accounts and finances. They were often family members or close friends of the patient. Sometimes a court appointed conservator other than a relative or a friend would be appointed.

In those days most of the cost of hospitalization was paid for by the state through Medi-Cal if the patient had no means of paying, which was often the case. Anyone who already was receiving monthly SSI checks would be billed accordingly. The financial status of a patient during hospitalization and after discharge was worked out by a social worker in coordination with federal and state programs. A person could agree to stay in the hospital voluntarily after any legal holds had expired. Some patients were admitted on a totally voluntary basis from the start. A lot of the patients with multiple admissions or who were chronic in nature were glad to be there. For many it was home and they never wanted to leave. These people usually ended up being transferred to a long term unit on a conservatorship or on a voluntary basis. A voluntary commitment was called a 6000.

Almost everyone has heard the term "5150". It has synonymously become an acronym for a crazy person on the loose or someone who is mentally disturbed. The police use it as one of their codes when out in the field. We used it every day on the unit. A 5150 for those of you who have not heard of it is a 72 hour involuntary hold placed on a person by qualified authorities, such as a police officer, if they are determined to be a danger to themselves, a danger to others or are gravely disabled. A 5250 is an additional 14 day hold that can be placed on a person if they continue to show signs of grave mental disability. Then the conservatorship process can be started after that period of time.

Today the laws regarding mental health treatment in California have changed a lot. The whole system developed to pay for treatment has shifted to the individual county's responsibility rather than the state. This was one of the reasons why some of the state hospitals were closed and also why we now see many people using emergency rooms and jails as treatments settings. The counties are often unwilling to pay for large numbers of acutely ill persons, thus forcing it onto the jails and emergency rooms. It further perpetuates a "revolving door" situation much like we had at the state hospital when I worked there. The LPS act also contained provisions for proper after care and placement of these people. The social worker's job was to work with local county facilities and to find places for them to live and to make sure that they received the care they needed. This included access to doctors, vocational training, physical therapy and food and clothing as examples. Thankfully at the time there were plenty of half way homes and board and care facilities in the surrounding counties, some good, some not.

Sadly though, many people didn't last long in these facilities. So many times they would decompose back into an unmanageable state and would return to the hospital where we would start the process all over again. Just like in convalescent hospitals and nursing homes, there is always that element of uncertainty regarding the quality of care received in these mostly for- profit businesses. If the staff at a board and care facility didn't make sure that a person was getting the medication that they desperately needed, this could easily trigger a relapse. I'm not saying that all of the people who ran these places were uncaring or neglectful, most of them were not. I spent many hours in board and care facilities during my training and I know how difficult it is to manage people who are generally, and often unfairly, considered to be social outcasts and are not wanted in the community.

I fondly remember one particular patient who had been admitted to our unit several times. He suffered from severe depression and had threatened suicide many times. His name was Louis. He was a small little curly-haired Jewish man who we all grew to feel a real compassion toward. The first time I met him was at one of the board and care homes where I was training during psych tech school. I think he really benefitted from his stays in the hospital and usually by the time he was transferred or discharged from our unit he seemed more on his feet and ready to give it another shot on the outside. He would say "I think I can do it this time." There was always a lot of hand shaking and hugging at his departure as he wiped away the tears from under his thin wire frame glasses. He was always placed in a half way home or board and care facility when he was not hospitalized.

The last time he was treated on our unit was a heartbreaking experience for some of us who had worked so closely with him. The doctor who had been assigned to Louis, for whatever reason, abruptly decided to discharge him back to the community, much to the dismay of the nursing staff, as we all felt that he was not ready to go back this time, that he needed more time. Louis was indeed discharged after his 72 hour hold was up. I think the doctor somehow thought that Louis was just playing the system and was using the "revolving door" problem as a reason to release him so quickly. We got a call two days after his discharge informing us that Louis had hanged himself off of a bridge. Some of us wept.

On Unit 77, as with all the units, we often based the treatment plan on a time frame. If the patient was admitted on a 5150 then we had 72 hours to treat the patient initially, not knowing whether or not they would be discharged or placed on another legal hold. If the patient was subsequently placed on a 14 day hold we could then adjust the treatment plan accordingly, and so on. Although the doctor had the authority to place a patient on a 5250 or to recommend a temporary conservatorship, the rest of the staff, yours truly included, often were asked for our evaluations and recommendations concerning the future of an individual. After all we were the ones who had the most direct contact with the patients, on a 24/7 basis.

It was almost impossible for someone committed on a 5150 to get released before the 72 hours were up. I only saw it happen once or twice. There was a powerful presence of the ACLU as well as personal attorneys representing certain patients. Family and friends were also a big part of determining the future status of someone committed on a 14 day hold or longer. A patient had the legal right to a Writ of Habeas Corpus and a portable courtroom was often set up on the hospital grounds to handle these cases. The law stated that a person must be granted the right to a trial under a Writ of Habeas Corpus within 30 days, but often times it was quicker than that. Sometimes we had to transport patients to the main courthouse in Ventura for their hearings.

If a patient could demonstrate that he or she was not a danger to themselves, a danger to others or gravely disabled at the time of the hearing, then the judge had the power to release the patient to the custody of family or friends. There were many times that we had family members pleading on behalf of their loved ones for them to be released. This was not always best for the patient and we drudged through many family conferences with multiple staff members present, trying to convince them that their relative really needed to stay in the hospital and continue treatment. There were those times when a judge would declare the person sane and release them on the spot. This often brought much consternation to our staff when we were informed of the decision. We always had a saying about that; that it was amazing how someone who was clearly psychotic and met all the criteria for hospitalization under the law was able to stand in front of a judge and convince him or her that they posed no immediate threats and were capable of taking care of all of their personal needs!

But that is the way it was. There were people who needed to be there for treatment without a doubt. There were people who really didn't need to be there at all. And there were people who were somewhere in between. That was the delicate balance that we worked with. Yes there were mistakes made. Yes there were times that a person should not have been prescribed certain medications. Yes there were snap judgement calls made. Yes there were practices that were called into question. And yes there were abuses. And yes we got it right, too. It is my humble opinion that without the dramatic intervention and treatment that was given at Camarillo State Hospital, in those days, tens of thousands of people would have been worse off or even dead.

The law made it clear that while a person was in the care of the state they must receive humane treatment and their physical needs must be met. For many patients a bed to sleep in and three meals a day were all they needed. We also went to great lengths to maintain good personal hygiene for our patients. We had large clean shower rooms, a barbershop, clean linen, clean clothing and a community dining room, shared by the three units in program 3A. We also had coffee available and smoking was permitted in the dayroom. It was not exactly a concentration camp, nor was it the Ritz Carlton. There were a couple of drinking fountains located in the hallways on the unit as well.

Photograph by Robert Inglis
Involuntary patients were locked behind doors like these

We had a patient once who was a chronically ill schizophrenic and one of his behaviors was to not stop drinking water at the fountain, if unsupervised. He would drink until his abdomen would swell to an enormous size. Too much water can cause a person's electrolytes to spin out of balance and can even cause death. He managed to elude us a couple of times. By the time we found him at the water fountain he had already bloated up to balloon proportions. Needless to say that after that we watched him like a hawk. He was eventually transferred off of the unit and I will never know if he eventually died as a result of this strange behavior that has been described in psychology textbooks.

Escorting all of the patients, or at least those who were able to attend, to the dining room was always a challenge. The food was fairly decent as I recall. It was always a well-balanced meal with all the food groups represented, including dessert. I remember many times when a patient would get out of control in the dining room and had to be physically removed and taken back to the unit, usually to receive a PRN and probably placed in a quiet room for a period of time. We had patients that gorged themselves and patients that wouldn't eat at all. Force feeding was occasionally done on a medical unit if the patient refused to eat for a long period of time. We usually had a few patients that had to remain on the unit, so we brought their trays of food back with us after the meal time was over. On a funny note, we sometimes fudged on the amount of trays we needed and ended up eating them ourselves in our employee break room on the unit. One time the head dining room person came onto the unit to see us about a special diet request, or something like that, and caught us red handed. It was really embarrassing and put an end to "free" meals.

So the laws pertaining to the treatment of all patients admitted to Camarillo State Hospital were clearly spelled out. We followed them closely. They were omnipresent. They became the common nomenclature that we so frequently used to document the care of the patient, right alongside medical charting terminology and doctor's orders. I can't imagine how it must have been in the days before the LPS act was enacted, when the patients were locked up and forgotten about so many times. I think it would have been very difficult and wrong to operate a large institution such as Camarillo State Hospital without proper legal guidelines to protect a person's basic rights and to ensure that they received humane care. It was indeed a time for change in 1973, when I knowingly and willingly burst onto the scene.

Photographs by Robert Inglis

How many people walked these hallways and staircases
and peered out of shuttered windows

CHAPTER 6
A Forceful Compromise

As a short detour I would like to talk just a little bit about some of my other experiences and thoughts and how they may relate to certain issues that have for so long been at the forefront of controversy at Camarillo State Hospital. After I left the state hospital and bounced around a bit I took up a short career at Ventura County Mental Health Department working in the in-patient unit. In many ways it was the same as Camarillo State hospital. The nursing procedures were very similar, the medications prescribed were virtually the same and the general patient mix was familiar to me. One of the big differences was that there were no locks on the doors. Patients admitted on a 5150 could easily walk away if they wanted to. There were two quiet rooms used for violent cases or when a person was considered a danger to themselves or others. We had to follow the same set of laws.

There was a separate team of people who went out into the community to respond to emergency calls. A person might call 911 or the county threatening suicide or someone might be actively hallucinating. Whatever the case the Medical Evaluation Team's or "METS" as they were referred to, job was to evaluate these people and make the determination as to whether or not they needed to be taken in to the in-patient unit, either voluntarily or involuntarily. On occasion I had the privilege of going out with the MET team when they were shorthanded. The MET team used cars fitted with heavy wire cages separating the front and back seats, very much like a police car. They also had a "license to fly" if necessary. It was quite an experience and gave me an insight into how a person may end up at the county or eventually transferred to the state hospital. A lot of times the situation or problem could be alleviated by talking to the individual or their family or spouse and leaving them with options, such as hotline phone numbers and information about county resources. Bringing someone in was usually a last resort. The police department was an integral part of this whole process as well.

Unfortunately police brutality in this country has been in the forefront for quite some time now. There have been so many instances played out on the national stage bringing into question the judgement and methods used by the police during encounters with individuals, especially black men. I'm not here to pass judgement on anyone. I just want to point out that even the highly trained law enforcement officers of this great nation make mistakes. They are often placed in a situation where decisions must be made in a split second. The elements of racial discrimination and profiling of certain individuals are brought up after the fact in so many cases. The media tends to sensationalize this kind of story to get higher ratings, whether or not the victim's rights were actually denied. The fact is that some of the officers do indeed violate a person's rights and react in an inappropriate manner, sometimes resulting in the death of someone. Sometimes the officer is in the right, having read the situation correctly and having acted in a professional manner that is acceptable, regardless of the outcome. There is a fine line that is drawn between the two.

When I worked for the county the police were often called to handle tough situations and to use force when it was necessary. The MET team worked hand and hand with the police. Almost every day we would see a patient brought in to in-patient by the police, usually in handcuffs. There were times when the patient definitely had been roughed up and showed signs of injuries due to a struggle with the police. It was all very well documented of course. At Camarillo State Hospital we didn't have the luxury of having the police available to handle these situations, it was just us.

Although there was that little hospital police department, they were not called upon to handle the day to day struggles on every unit in the hospital. The place was just too big. They were mainly there to be traffic cops and sometimes called as back-up when there was a desperate situation unfolding, like the time the mace was deployed in the courtyard and I had gotten it in my eyes. They were also used when there was an

AWOL patient that needed to be located and brought back to the unit.

I have already mentioned in this story some of the methods that we used at Camarillo on a daily basis to help control violent people, people who were acting out, people who were a danger to others. There were four main recourses that we had available to us. One was medicating the individual, using heavy tranquilizers. One was using leather cuffs and belts, an equivalent to handcuffs. One was putting someone in a quiet room or "side room". And one was simply physical force used by the staff to subdue and restrain someone. These methods were often used in conjunction with each other. There were also panic buttons in every nursing station that could be pushed, alerting neighboring units of a situation. We used the panic button regularly as it would send six or eight testosterone-filled male employees flying in from every direction ready to do whatever it took.

We were trained to use a mattress to force a patient into the corner of a room so he or she could not escape. This minimized injuries but was awkward and didn't always work. We were trained how to lay someone down on the floor in the proper manner. We were trained how to apply cuff and belt restraints and even how to safely tie someone into a bed, if needed. A patient who had been placed in cuff and belts had very little mobility, about as much as a prisoner in a chain gang would. Cuff and belt restraints were only used as a last resort and they were generally not kept on for long periods. Believe it or not strait jackets were never used the entire time I was there, at least I never saw one used. It was an unwritten rule that male employees were always the ones who handled the physical restraining. Female employees were there, they were right there, but they were usually the ones who had the needle and syringe in hand ready to slam a #1 into the upper outer quadrant. After all, this was the 1970's and gender equality was just beginning to become an issue, politically speaking.

The drugs that were used in the state hospital at that time to treat and to tranquilize patients varied widely, depending on the diagnosis and the disposition of the patient. Each doctor had his or her own ideas about which drugs to use, how often and for how long. But like I said before, almost all of the patients were given some form of medication. It has long been debated as to whether or not these drugs were used in mental institutions for actual treatment of the patient or whether they were indiscriminately used to keep everyone tranquilized and in a "zombie" state. I don't think that argument was ever settled. It has also been argued whether or not these drugs actually benefit people, whether they work as intended or just mask someone's symptoms.   The fact is that the use of heavy tranquilizers was a necessity and not an option for many of the patients.

The medication room on the unit was fully stocked at all times. We regularly filled out requisition forms and made trips to the pharmacy to fill them. We were also fully stocked up on first aid supplies and medical necessities such as bandages, dressings, swabs, ointments and alcohol and peroxide. It was very complete. Medications were given out three times a day for the majority of the patients. PRN's and STAT orders were done when required. There was a medication cart with three shelves on it. All of the medications were placed in paper or plastic cups. Most were in pill form, some liquid. The cups were lined up on each shelf with the patient's name, medication and dose clearly labeled on each patient's med card. When it was time to pass out medications all the patients were made to stand in a single line all the way down the hallway. We usually had two staff members present, one to hand out the medication and one to pass out little cups of water to take it with. I got pretty good at setting up the medications and passing them out. All of the psych techs took turns in the med room. We always had to make sure that the patient actually swallowed the medication, as many were very reluctant and complained about how it made them feel.

There are a number of anti-psychotic drugs that were used. Most of these are in the family of drugs called phenothiazines. A list of these drugs that were commonly used includes Thorazine, Mellaril, Stelazine, Haldol, Serentil, Prolixin, Permitil, Compazine (also used to treat nausea) and others. Before phenothiazines were discovered early drugs used to treat mental illness were meant to induce sleep. These included alcohol and later pain killers and barbiturates. Minor tranquilizers like Valium and Librium were used for anxiety and also for tremors in alcoholic patients. Phenobarbital and Dilantin were used for Epileptics and patients with seizure disorders. Lithium was used to treat Manic-Depressive Disorder (now called Bi-Polar Disorder). We frequently had to take patients who were on Lithium to the lab for blood tests to monitor the lithium levels in their system, as too much can be very dangerous. Elavil and similar drugs were given to people with non-psychotic depression to elevate their mood. Artane and Cogentin was used to prevent EPS, or Extrapyramidal Side Effects, from some of the heavy tranquilizers. EPS can be marked by severe muscle contractions and/or Parkinson like movements. Insulin was frequently given to diabetic patients subcutaneously. We also used a fair amount of heavy pain killers such as Darvon and Codeine. A lot of Benadryl and Robitussin was given for cold and sinus problems and Amoxicillin and Penicillin was widely used for infections and respiratory problems of all kinds. Multi-vitamins were given to most patients. Sustacal was prescribed for underweight or malnourished patients. Mineral oil was often given to patients who were constipated, one of the side effects of taking these medications. There was also a large amount of Tylenol and aspirin used for fever and minor pain, and of course good old MOM (milk of magnesia).

The med room was also stocked with every injectable form of medication, intramuscular, subcutaneous and intravenous. We had disposable syringes ready to go and we also had every gauge of needle and every size of syringe at our disposal. Psych techs are not licensed to give IV's so we left that up to the people who were licensed to do that, such as an R.N. or a phlebotomist. That was not a problem as there was usually always someone around who could run an IV. On more than one occasion I witnessed as a lab tech would struggle to draw blood from and uncooperative patient, resulting in severe bruising of the arm.

So we were well equipped to administer medications and treat patients for physical problems like cuts, abrasions, burns, rashes and infections as well as malnutrition and dehydration. We were well versed in medical terminology and charting procedures. We were frequently ordered to monitor a patient and record their blood pressure, temperature, pulse and respirations, as well as performing q15 (every 15 minutes) checks on suicidal patients or patients with pressing medical issues. I&O's (intake and output of liquids and solids) were ordered by the doctor when warranted. We were sometimes required to insert catheters, give lavage treatments and enemas. We were fully trained and certified in CPR. We also had the medical/surgical unit in the same complex available if a patient required intensive care or emergency surgery or treatment for broken bones and other serious injuries.

Contrary to what the general public may or may not have thought about the level of care that could potentially be given to patients confined in a large mental institution, it was very professional and every effort was made to ensure the well-being and safety of these individuals. Nothing was done illegally or on purpose to harm any person as far as the dispensing of any medication or the treating of any medical conditions to my knowledge.

At any time while we were on duty the potential for violence to occur or a situation getting out of control was very real. Many patients walking around on the unit, especially new admissions, were unpredictable. Sometimes all we knew about someone was the fact that they were there and what was contained in their initial intake chart. It is very hard to get reliable or factual information out of a person who is highly agitated, resistive or out of touch with reality.

As I stated earlier all patients were first screened through the main admissions facility and then transferred to one of the units. They would always get a very brief physical exam by a physician, if possible, and a psychiatric evaluation. If they were brought in by the police they might have had an arrest record or a police evaluation in their chart. If they were being re-admitted their previous chart may have been brought with them as well. The average time they were in admitting was very brief usually. In other words we were usually seeing them in the most acute stage of their illness at that point, from the time they walked onto our unit.

Photograph by Robert Inglis
Outside View of Typical Unit

If a patient was admitted on the evening shift or the night shift the staff had to follow the intake doctor's orders until they could be further evaluated by our own doctors and staff. This also pertained to weekends. There were on call doctors for after hours for the entire hospital available if we needed to get a STAT order or permission for something. Most of these doctors were reluctant to even step foot onto the units and would give verbal orders over the phone. They were forced to come onto the unit if a patient had incurred a severe injury and needed to be seen by a doctor, such as needing stitches or if they were having convulsions or epileptic seizures.

I think it was mid-morning on the day shift one day and there were several of us going about our business in the nursing station, making phone calls, charting, compiling documents, etc. I believe it was myself, Gill, Margaret Garrison, and maybe Kathy Taylor. There were always people coming and going. We had just received a rather wild and unpredictable man who was running around the unit causing a lot of commotion. We didn't quite know what to make of him. We had been keeping a close watch on him and as I recall we had obtained a PRN order from one of the doctors in case we needed to tranquilize him. We usually always left the door to the nursing station open, even though patients were not encouraged to come in there unless we requested them to.

As I was casually talking to one of my co-workers I happened to glance up just when this wiry little character was running at full speed from the end of the long hallway heading straight for the nursing station. You could see the wild, blank look in his eyes as he went airborne. We only had a split second to react as he crashed with full force into the nursing station. Office chairs and filing cabinets went flying and toppling all over the place. Coffee cups, papers, pens, charts, and books were strewn about. We all managed to get out of the way, barely. He came to a stop when he smashed right into Margaret Garrison's desk at the very end of the nursing station. She was huddled in the small corner next to her desk and was visibly shaken. I yelled for some back up and the individual was subdued and placed in a side room and given a PRN. The patient miraculously escaped any serious injury and we were all ok.

There were only a few times that I can remember being scared, really scared. One of those times still haunts me to this day. A very large, extremely muscular man in his twenties had been admitted on a 5150 to our unit during the night. He was obviously very agitated and suspicious of everyone and everything. He had come from one of the rougher parts of LA and Angel Dust was the suspected cause of his paranoid behavior, and subsequent hospitalization. This was a scary looking dude and we were all keeping our distance. He had a set of bongo drums in his possession when admitted and no one was going to tell him he couldn't have them. The bongo drums had a shoulder strap and he carried them around with him at all times.

It was on the third day of the 72 hour hold that he began to escalate even further. Whatever medication he had been prescribed was not working yet. He had not physically threatened anyone up to that point but you just got the feeling that something was about to happen.

We tried to calm him down by assuring him that he was there for a good reason and that we were all concerned about him and only had good intentions. Ron Wallace, the shift lead, went to talk to the doctor about the situation and came back with a stat order for a #1. The injection was prepared in the med room and we approached the patient with caution. I said "We have a shot for you that will make you feel much better, can we give it to you?" He said something like "That's bullshit, you ain't givin' me nothin'" It was at that moment that he started to approach us as if he really wanted to hurt someone. One of us shouted to the ladies in the nursing station to hit the panic button and jump on the phone.

The back-ups arrived just in time. There were ten of us and one of him. Dr. Swiner was called and came running down the hallway. Ok, this was it. We all jumped on top of the patient. I was the first one to make physical contact with him and his set of bongo drums went crashing down on the floor as a result. Sadly the bongo drums were broken in the process. As we piled on top of him we found out that he had the strength of several men, maybe as much as all ten of us. We had always heard that Angel Dust can manifest this in people, but now we knew it was true. We could barely hold him down. Every time we thought we had this very strong man pinned down he would buck up and throw some of us off as if we weighed nothing. Dr. Swiner held out his arm and signaled Mary to hand him the syringe. There was no way we were going to get his pants down far enough to give the shot properly. Normally when you give an IM in the buttocks it is given in the upper outer quadrant and you always aspirate the syringe to make sure you are not drawing blood. Dr. Swiner simply slammed the needle right through his jeans without aspirating. He was an experienced emergency room doctor and it showed.

It took several minutes of us holding the patient down before the medication started to take effect. He could see that his bongo drums were broken and knew that I had caused it, at least that is what he kept saying. He said he was going to kill me when he got the chance. After the drugs took effect and he was heavily tranquilized he was placed in a quiet room. We all shook it off and composed ourselves. What an experience!

I spent the rest of the day and all that evening at home thinking about what would happen between him and me. It just happened that my days off started the next day. When I came back to work from my days off I was relieved to find out that the patient had been discharged. The combination of the Angel Dust in his system wearing off and the tranquilizing effects from the medication he was receiving brought him way back down to reality. I sincerely hope that he was able to stay off drugs and live a good life. We never saw him again.

The issue of whether or not excessive force or abuse of patients actually occurred within the confines of the state hospital is somewhat subjective in terms of how you would define it and whether any or part of it was justified. That being said I want to lay it out there, yes there were abuses and there was excessive force used at times. It was never condoned or done sadistically as far as I know. I think in almost every instance it was a visceral reaction by the individual or individuals involved. The story I told about the large, scary man that took ten people to subdue demonstrates how quickly these situations can unfold and the decisions that must be made in order to avoid a potentially dangerous outcome.

I myself used excessive force out of necessity on more than one occasion, as did many of the people I worked with.

I got to know a lot of the other techs that worked on the adjoining units to ours. We all worked closely together and, like I said, responded quickly when needed. We also took turns working overtime on the other units so everybody knew everybody, so to speak. One of the guys that worked on Unit 80 was a tough street fighter who had grown up on the streets of Oxnard and had become a fairly well known boxer. He had a reputation of being someone you wouldn't want to tangle with, a fierce Mexican-American man with a Golden Gloves belt. He was great to work with and everyone admired him. When he was around there was a feeling of security. We had his back and he had ours.

The first time I worked with Ray was on Unit 80 when I was doing an overtime shift. We got to talking and he invited me into the barber shop to continue the conversation. He opened a little refrigerator in the corner of the room and pulled out a couple of ice cold beers. "Here, have a beer" he said. I was a little shocked but took the beer nonetheless and drank it down with him. He said that he always kept a stash of brews on hand and that everyone knew about it. I said "Cool". It was not a secret that some of the employees might drink a beer or two while on their lunch breaks, no big deal. I got to know Ray pretty well and considered him a friend.

A couple of the other male techs on my unit and I had to respond to a situation on Unit 80 one day. We ran down the hall and through Unit 78 and into Unit 80. Upon arriving we saw Ray standing over a male patient who was laying on the floor, covered in blood and obviously beaten up very badly. The whole situation was one of confusion and amazement at all of the blood. We managed to pick up the almost lifeless body of the patient and take him to a room for initial treatment and observation. He had several large lacerations on his face and his eyes were swollen shut, almost as if he had been on the losing end of a fierce fifteen round title fight. Ray was visible shaken but seemed Ok otherwise.

Apparently the male patient, who had been showing signs of paranoia and agitation, snuck up behind Ray and landed a devastating sucker punch to the side of Ray's head. Ray was staggered at first and then, after regaining his composure, proceeded to mop the floor with the patient, resulting in some serious injuries. The doctor on duty stitched up the wounds and we cleaned the patient up as best we could. As far as I can remember the incident reports that were filled out by the staff and the attending doctor were written in a way that placed almost all of the blame on the patient, stating that the employee had responded in self-defense. The patient was injured severely by a hospital employee but was it abuse or self-defense? Personally I think Ray should have stopped sooner than he did but he was assaulted first. The patient definitely did not deserve to be beaten to within an inch of his life. The patient was transferred to medical and fully recovered, but he probably had some scars for life.

The use of "choke holds" is probably one of the most contentious and talked about subjects pertaining to the history of patient abuse at Camarillo State Hospital. Let me say right here and now that it did occur. I personally applied choke holds on several occasions. Although I never saw any patients who were seriously injured, or died, as a result of this type of excessive force, it did happen. A "choke hold" is when a person is approached from behind and the forearm of the approaching person is placed on the neck of the individual. Compression is applied by grasping the forearm and hand with the other hand and pulling back forcefully, essentially shutting off air supply to the individual. The result is submission. The patient would usually slump to the floor, sometimes gasping for breath, sometimes becoming unconscious, until they once again were breathing normally.

I don't remember exactly how many times I employed this type of restraint or how many times I saw someone else do it. I don't even remember the names or faces of any of those patients. My memory is cloudy, almost as if it is blocked out of my conscience. Why do I still remember many specific patients and their names but not in these cases, I really don't know. I do know that in every case it was a matter of security or self-defense and that the safety of myself or others was probably in danger. There was never, to my knowledge, any personal malice toward these individuals. There was no sadistic desire to harm them or to endanger their lives. It was done for a very obvious reason, to prevent someone from potentially harming others. A comparison would be like when a police officer puts a baton under the chin of a suspect to control them physically.

The use of choke holds, I believe, was widespread throughout the hospital while I worked there. It was not documented and not talked about outside the hospital. It was, sadly, the most effective way to subdue patients who were violent, dangerous, uncooperative, and unpredictable. I don't think anyone wanted to do it, but as I learned so early on, it was the way things were done when you couldn't wait for back up. It was one of those things that was passed down from year to year. I can only guess how long this technique had been used at

Camarillo State hospital, and for that matter all over the country. The technique itself, although very effective, should never have been used in the first place. The fact that we had little or nothing to protect ourselves, in many cases, should have been addressed by the administration and other viable means should have been adopted. I don't feel good about the fact that I was a part of this, but at the time a person didn't give it that much thought; it was sadly a necessary evil. People can draw their own conclusions but unless they could have put themselves into our shoes it is very hard to say how any particular person would have reacted under those circumstances. That all changed in 1976 when Michael Bradbury, Ventura County District Attorney, opened an investigation into nearly 100 mysterious deaths at Camarillo State Hospital, spanning a number of years.

This resulted in a grand jury inquisition and many hospital employees ended up testifying. I somehow was not subpoenaed. Ron Wallace, the day shift lead testified as well as several other people from our program. There were technicians, nurses and doctors from all over the hospital brought to the stand. It was all very hush hush at the time, and no one who had to testify would talk about it. The 100 deaths were by no means all said to be because of using illegal choke holds, but for a variety of accusations, such as deaths as a result of being overmedicated by tranquilizers or physical neglect.

You can go online and read various accounts, some of them lengthy, about specific incidents and certain patients' deaths. There are accounts of supposed deaths due to overdoses using the #1 cocktail and from choke holds. There is some mention of grand jury testimony as well. Ron Wallace was the only person on the stand that admitted that he had heard about the use of choke holds but took the Fifth Amendment when asked if he had personally done it or had seen anyone else do it. Honestly, I don't know what I would have said or admitted to if I were sitting on the hot seat like some of the people I knew and worked with.

The investigation and subsequent grand jury inquisition came to an end with several indictments, including some doctors, but no convictions or jail time, as far as I know. The use of choke holds and other methods for restraining patients pretty much stopped after that. Was the fact that over 100 patients' deaths that were never fully explained justified? Of course not. It was a tragedy. It will go down in history as a dark time in mental health treatment. It has been rumored that the Eagles 1977 "Hotel California" was a reference to Camarillo State Hospital.

CHAPTER 7
The Desire to Connect

It was somewhere around the same time, about two years after I started work, when a couple of important changes came to pass on Unit 77. One: I took the test to become a Psychiatric Technician 1, and two: we went from being an all-male unit to a co-ed unit with equal amounts of male and female patients. I somehow passed the test with flying colors and placed first at Camarillo and third in the state and soon became the AM Shift Lead after Ron Wallace left to take a job in program management. It was perfect timing for me and I was very excited to say the least. Those "people" up in Sacramento decided that going co-ed was the wave of the future so we all geared up for the big change.

So I still had to answer to Margaret Garrison but now I had authority over everyone else on the day shift nursing staff. I kind of went through a self-metamorphosis in that I not only had to learn all of the supervisory duties that I was required to do, but my new position allowed me to become a more integral part of the treatment team. Surprisingly it was a fairly easy transition for me. I became very efficient at running certain day to day operations such as scheduling, running meetings and providing the doctors with everything they needed. Weekly I would call an all unit meeting in the dayroom, with patients and staff present, to orient new patients and inform every one of pertinent issues and procedures. A soon as the doctors arrived in the morning I would run a pile of charts up to their offices and individually sit down with them, along with the social workers to go over important issues regarding the patients' treatment plans and to discuss their conditions. The unit supervisor was, on the other hand, less hands on and was more of a liaison between the unit and the program offices and the hospital administration. The whole system worked as well as it should have, I suppose.

Converting to a co-ed unit was challenging at first but after a period of time we all got used to it. One side of the unit was male and the other side was female. Male patients were not allowed in the female rooms and vice versa. There was only one large shower room so we had to assign times for the men and the women. The male staff would supervise the shower room when it was the men's turn to shower and the female staff would supervise the women. One of the biggest concerns from the start was how in the hell were we going to keep males and females separated. Even mentally ill people have sexual desires and since we had all age groups of patients it was difficult at times to keep them apart. On more than one occasion we caught people in the bushes in the courtyard going at it. I don't think that we had any pregnancies as a result of these unions, at least none that I knew of.

I must say that having a unit with both sexes represented not only made it more interesting but we all got to experience firsthand how mental illness manifested itself in women, as we were so used to working with only men. I found out that women can be just as crazy or just as disturbed as men, maybe even more so in some cases. To this day I have many shocking memories of some of the female patients who graced our presence inside the walls of Unit 77.

Although many of the patients were not really capable of responding to individual or group therapy, we did have enough who we thought would possibly benefit from it. We had regular group therapy sessions on the unit. Group or individual therapy was integrated into the treatment plan along with medication. The aim of group therapy, in theory, is fairly straightforward. It allows group members to share their strengths and make people feel that they are a part of something. It also can allow a person to explore his or her own problems and relate them to the group through common experience. Hopefully the person can learn and grow as a result.

There has been much discussion over whether group therapy is actually effective. My personal opinion is that it can be effective in people who are capable of understanding the purpose of it and can take it seriously. In these individuals it can, and does, strike a deep emotional chord sometimes, perhaps clearing the way or opening a door to an insight into themselves that they so desperately need.

Dr. Ellison, the unit psychologist, was a big believer in group and individual psychotherapy. He spent many hours doing one-on-one sessions with some of the most disturbed people that you will ever see. He also ran the group therapy sessions with a professionalism that was very impressive. All of the things that I mentioned in the above principles of psychotherapy were practiced and evident in his self-proclaimed "chaotic" approach. Sometimes the sessions were "Psychodrama" like in nature, with a heavy emphasis on the protagonist role. I learned a lot about psychotherapy during those years. There were times when things got so intense, when the emotions were so high and the tears and crying were so real that we were emotionally drained afterward. There was always a lot of finger pointing and accusing of fellow group members. It was not uncommon for a patient to leap out of his or her chair and lunge at another group member.

I profoundly remember the many patients I saw with scars running all the way up the inside of their forearms from either attention getting stunts or actual suicide attempts. Again, this is one of those fine line areas where it may be hard to tell if someone is genuinely suicidal or not. It can start out more innocently with only light scratches on the arms or legs, with the person covering up with long sleeves to conceal it from others, but sometimes can escalate into a much more serious situation. I can only surmise as to how many of these people died as a result of their valiant struggles with life itself. I do know one thing though, and that is that almost all of them were young and that a large percentage were female. I remember sitting in the circle one day when the doctor introduced one of our new female patients to the rest of the group. She had the telltale razorblade scars on both arms from her many attempts. She was reluctant to participate at first, as so many are, but eventually broke down after several days and was able to talk about some of her most guarded inner demons to those around her. She became so tearful at one point that she fell to the floor, crying and sobbing uncontrollably. Some members of the group rushed to her side and attempted to console her but she had to be taken back to her room and given a PRN. The next day she managed to find a piece of glass and slashed her wrist deeply. She was rushed to the medical unit where they treated her wound and sewed up her arm with many stitches. She was only eighteen years old.

Self-mutilation among adolescent females, as I said, was not uncommon for us to encounter. There are many reasons why a person may want to harm themselves in this manner. Young people exhibiting this type of behavior probably have a history of emotional trauma or sexual abuse and may have come from a dysfunctional family. They might also have eating disorders and may be obsessive compulsive or they may simply be encountering problems with their own peers and need a way to release their frustration. They can become highly emotional and uncontrollable at times. This type of patient was very difficult to treat effectively and by the time they were admitted to the state hospital they were usually in serious trouble. The fact that for many of them self-mutilation was the only way they knew to cry out for help or get someone to notice them was very sad because sometimes they went too far.

There were times when we were called upon to perform other duties outside of the unit, such as working in the medical records room or supervising at the pool, etc. Every unit took turns supplying staff members to do these jobs. I can vividly recall one occasion when I had to help out in the morgue; washing down, toe tagging, gowning and preparing the fresh corpse of a very young female from another unit who bled- out from cutting her wrists. I remember looking at her naked body lying on a table with her scarred wrists and forearms from previous suicide attempts clearly visible. Her otherwise young, healthy body looked simply asleep. When we finished working on her and slid her into the refrigerated body compartment and locked the stainless steel door, I felt a deep sadness come over me. I thought to myself "What a shame."

Teenage suicide and depression was only one of the many problems that we saw and attempted to deal with in these group settings. I was privileged to have had the opportunity to lead the group on several occasions. I learned a lot about myself in the process. The art of leading with questions and knowing when to let a person spill out and when to control the situation with a more steady hand is that of the doctor or therapist. I got just a little taste of that. Dr. Ellison was always there to take control if a session got out of control and he would always try to de-escalate the group before they returned to their rooms. He loved to share his knowledge and, as I talked about earlier in the book, was the one who got in trouble for trying to teach some of us the secrets of reading Rorschach tests.

Since we were a relatively short term unit, and because it was a fairly small percentage of the unit population who could realistically benefit from a group setting, we often were not able to see real, concrete results, as far as the effect of group therapy and long term medication regimens were concerned. The patients were either discharged or transferred to a long term unit. I guess we could all feel good about the fact that we did the best we could with the time we had and the tools we had at our disposal.

We had a great recreational therapist, Bob Rodriguez, who had a large room at one end of the unit filled with every kind of painting, sculpting, crafts, music, dance and movement activities you could imagine. He worked with the patients in developing motor skills and improving social and cognitive functioning in an effort to prepare them for life outside the hospital. Sometimes the technicians would spend time with some of their assigned patients in the recreational therapy room. This type of therapy in many ways was very effective in alleviating anxiety and aggressiveness in many patients. It also was therapeutic for people who were withdrawn or depressed. I have nothing but good things to say about the whole concept of this form of therapy, and like a good group therapy session, it can definitely boost confidence and raise the spirits of many of these people.

So in between all of the commotion and the violence and the chaos that was so much a part of everyday life on the unit, we also tried to provide a real therapeutic environment which was conducive to treating each patient on an individual basis, with one goal in mind, to get better. I can't say that we succeeded as much as we wanted to. The failure rate and the possibility that we would see someone over and over again was fairly high. The fact that we were treating people with a wide variety of illnesses and from all adult age groups, male and female, in an environment such as the confines of Camarillo State Hospital, dramatically reduced the chances, in many cases, for success. But we won a few.

When a patient left the unit there was always a follow up plan as to where they would go, where they would live, how they could access money and how they could take care of their everyday needs. The hard working social workers on our unit made every effort to see that the patients were well set up with follow-up doctor visits and access to medication as well as a roof over their heads and food to eat. Many patients were on conservatorships. The conservator was legally responsible for making sure that all these needs were met. If the patient was sent to a longer term unit for further treatment, then their financial and legal status would be handled by the social workers on the unit they were transferred to.

So hopefully you can see how the whole approach - the medication, the therapy, the physical well-being and the follow up after discharge was called the treatment plan. That is what we did, and with the exception of some of the negative history that is so inextricably attached, we did it well. The contemporaneous methods that we used in those days may not be on par with modern day treatment standards but it was the world in which we lived and the doctrine to which we subscribed.

If you were able to look out of the eyes of a patient who has been hospitalized in a mental institution, or perhaps if you yourself were one of those patients, then you might look at the whole experience completely different than that of the nurse or the doctor. You might point out that the staff was indifferent and cold or that they were neglectful and careless. You might also say that it did you no good to be in there. You might have been scared and anxious and even fearful of your life. Or, you might feel that you actually received the help that you so desperately needed, at the time, in order to bring you back from the abyss or prevent you from doing something harmful to yourself or someone else. Each person is different and each person deals with intervention in their own way. There have been many accounts written by people who have been treated in a mental hospital setting or who have been institutionalized. It is important to listen to their stories too. There are definitely two sides to every coin. Myself, I can only look out of my own eyes and tell you how and what I saw.

CHAPTER 8
A Day in the Life

I take the last drag off of my cigarette and put it out in the tall ash tray just outside the door. I reach down and grab the big set of keys dangling from my belt and insert the A key into the lock. As it clicks and as I begin to open the door I can already hear the all too familiar sounds of the unit as it is waking up. I can hear doors opening and closing and the faint sound of toilets flushing. The groans and shrieks that are automatically built into this environment echo throughout the hallways. As I walk past the patient dormitories to the left and right of me I glance into each room to get a visual assessment. Many patients are still sleeping, with the security of the heavy gray state issue blankets tightly wrapped around them, while others are getting dressed and some are attempting to make their beds. Is everything ok here? Do I see any new faces that might have arrived in the middle of the night or the evening before? I finish the walk up the long hallway and arrive at the door to the nursing station. There are already several staff members there from the night shift and the day shift standing around talking, drinking coffee and waiting for the change of shift meeting. I can tell that the night shift is anxious to go home, with that "Let's get this show on the road" look on their faces. Jenny, one of the night shift technicians, who wore army boots and heavy men's clothing, reached into her jacket pocket, pulled out her tobacco pipe and lit it up. I chuckle to myself because she was probably the first "butch dike" character I had ever seen and I say "Good morning everyone".

It's 7:30 in the morning and as soon as everyone is assembled we have a quick change of shift meeting. There were two new admissions during the PM shift. One is a young woman suffering from depression and devoid of many social skills that we take for granted. She had been increasingly not able to take care of her own basic needs. She was admitted after her family called the mental health department for help and they recommended that she be transferred to Camarillo State for possible long term treatment. The other is a schizophrenic man in his forties who was highly agitated and possibly hallucinating upon admission and is now resting quietly in one of the side rooms. We are told that he received a #1 around 2100 and had not stirred since. We get a general run down from the night staff about the rest of the unit population and how the shift went. They report that one of the male patients got out of bed and became agitated at two in the morning and was given a PRN and put back in his bed with no further incidents. They changed the bandage on another patient who had an infection on his leg. Other than that it was a normal evening.

At 8 o'clock we go around to each room and yell out the "come to breakfast" call. Most all of the patients slowly make their way up the hallway, on the east side of the unit, to the dining room. Some patients need to be prodded and sometimes physically forced to attend while others are eager to eat. The dining room was a long rectangular room with no windows to speak of, with tables placed between two aisles leading to the front serving area. The patients formed two single file lines. Behind the counter were the food service employees who filled and handed out the trays of food. On the sides of the counter there was the silverware, cups, napkins and pitchers of water, milk, orange juice and coffee, along with all of the condiments needed for that particular meal. We made sure everyone got their food and that everyone found a place to sit.

We also waited on the patients, refilling their drinks, making sure they got everything they needed and offered seconds if there was enough left over, and there usually was. Many of the patients wanted seconds, and even thirds. Others would not eat at all. With the wide variety of patients we had and their given mental statuses it was always an adventure to get through a meal without any incidents. We usually had all of the available staff, with the exception of the person who was setting up the morning medications and the unit supervisor, in attendance to chaperone, assist the food service people and keep the peace. On many occasions we were seeing a patient for the first time at breakfast. Many of them were very skeptical of their surroundings and some, who were in a full blown paranoid state, were literally dangerous and needed to be treated with kid gloves. I can remember several times when we had to tackle a patient to the floor as food trays were flying everywhere. For others it was the best time of the day.

With all of the patients back on the unit and breakfast behind us it is time to get going with the rest of the day. The doctors and social workers arrive at 9 am. I begin setting up the new intake charts for the doctors to review and check with the unit supervisor to see if she needs me to do anything for her. "Yes Mark, we have three patients that need to go to the lab this morning. Can you get Kathy or George to take them? The appointment is at 10:15." "No problem Margaret. I'll take care of it. Anything else?" She says "No, except that I will be gone from one to three today for a program meeting; just make sure everything runs smoothly." I think to myself "God, not another fucking program meeting. All she does is go to program meetings!"

At 0900 it is medication time. We go again from room to room and summon everyone to line up single file. Jean Winters is assigned to the med room today. She wheels out the medication cart and places it just outside the med room door facing the long hallway leading to the center of the unit. Everything is set up and ready to go as each patient steps up to receive their oral medications. Of course there is always that percentage of patients who refuse to take their meds. In that case we would take the medication to them in their room and persuade them to take it or if all else failed the patient would receive an injection against their will. It all goes smoothly today. Passing out meds usually takes about a half an hour or so.

Soon after the meds are passed out the patient in the side room is waking up from the PRN. Gill and I open the big heavy door to take a peek at what we have. I see a man with a small build dressed in ragged clothing and no shoes. He has a full beard and wild hair. He appears to be very disheveled and lacking in any hygiene. As he begins to stir he looks around his surroundings in the confinement of the small room he is in and realizes that we are looking at him. He has a wild, crazy look in his eyes. "Hello. How are you feeling? Do you know where you are? You are in a hospital because you are having some problems," I say. There is no response from him. At this point he doesn't seem to be an imminent threat to anyone so we decide to assign him a bed and go from there. I will put his chart on the top of the stack for the doctor to review.

During the course of the morning many patients take turns showering, grooming and dressing. The men's and women's restrooms only had about six toilets each and I think the men's had four urinals. The shower room and the restrooms were a very busy place in the mornings as you could imagine. Given the nature of our patients, in general, there were many "indiscretions", so to speak, that occurred in the restrooms. I guess it was not that bad however, considering the foul conditions in many public restrooms I have run across in my life. About once a week housekeeping would come onto the unit to clean the showers and the restrooms as well as mop the floors and do other basic cleaning of the unit. They would pick up the dirty laundry and restock our linen closets with fresh towels and bedding. The rest of the time we had to perform all of the cleaning duties as needed.

It's almost 10 am. We have two discharges today. I hastily get their charts ready along with the others and head up the hall to the two doctors' offices. Dr. Samphan's office is on the right and Dr. Swiner's is on the left. I place the charts on both of their desks and wait for the rest of the staff to show up. As soon as we are all gathered we meet with one doctor, then the other. The discharge orders are signed by the doctors and I run the charts back down to the nursing station so the techs can complete the paperwork prior to them leaving the unit. We go over a few things and then begin to discuss the new patients. As soon as our morning meeting ends we will bring the female patient to Dr. Samphan's office so he can give her a quick physical examination, evaluate her mental status and prescribe accordingly. We will also try to do the same thing with the crazy-eyed man who had been in the side room. Something tells me that Dr. Swiner may have to do a bedside visit today.

At a little after 11 am I sit down in the nursing station and finish putting together the new admissions' charts. Every chart contained a section for doctors' orders, nurses' charting, vital signs, dietary needs, clinics, lab results and about twenty other unnecessary forms that the state made us fill out, such as multiple choice questions and "On a scale of 1 to 10 how would you rate this....." forms. Each of the nursing staff had an equal number of patients assigned to them. They were responsible for maintaining the chart and keeping it current and up to date.

I always loved medical charting for some reason. I don't know if it was because of the medical abbreviations that we frequently used like PO for by mouth, NPO for nothing by mouth, As Tol for as tolerated, BR for bathroom, a C with a line over it for with and an S with a line over it for without, BP TPR for blood pressure, temperature, pulse and respiration, OD, BID, TID, QID for how many times a day, H/O for history of, N/V for nausea and vomiting, R/O for rule out, and so on; or whether it was because of the words we used to describe the patients general condition and mental status. Words like agitated, aggressive, confused, withdrawn, uncooperative and hallucinating were the bread and butter of psychiatric charting. We also used other words and phrases like "resting quietly" or "remains agitated" or "pacing about". The verb "seems" was very frequently used. Almost every nurse or technician would write things like "He seems to be less agitated today" or "She seems less confused today."

I can look out of the windows in the nursing station and see the activities going on in the courtyard as well as the day room. Dr. Ellison is outside engaged in a vigorous volleyball game with his selected group of patients, and all seems well in the dayroom where the usual crappy daytime TV shows are on but only a few are paying any attention . Down the hall our recreational therapist is no doubt working with several people. That room is always interesting to go into to see all of the artwork and clay sculptures that the patients have done. Among the scores of drawings and paintings that are pinned or taped on the walls are that of various patients and staff members as well as some self-portraits. Some of them are twisted and bizarre and some of them are actually very good.

Outside view of Unit 77 dayroom

Old Unit 77 courtyard entrance as it looks today

The barber shop on the unit is open today and several patients are getting haircuts and shaves. We have been lucky lately because one of our patients is a retired hair stylist and he insists on cutting hair while he is here. He was hospitalized for depression and he says that it helps keep his mind off of his problems. He even styled one of our social worker's hair and she was delighted with the results. He did a lot better job than we did, that's for sure.

It seemed like the nursing station was the center of the universe for not only us but for many of the patients as well. All day long and all evening long, for that matter, patients would come and go. They had many requests such as cigarettes, coffee, extra food, extra blankets and a whole myriad of other things. Some would want to talk about their legal status or their plans after they were discharged. Others would simply wander into the nursing station to show off their bizarre behavior.

I remember a notably psychotic patient, Mark Thompson, who we had on more than one occasion, who had a compulsion to draw boxes and different shapes in the air with his fingers, in between sentences, as he was talking to you. He would look you dead in the eye after drawing a series of shapes and seemed to want a response from us or at least an acknowledgement letting him know that we understood what it meant. Of course it didn't mean anything to us but for him it was his way of interacting with other people. For some reason he felt the need to hover about the door to the nursing station and to draw as much attention as he could from the staff and from other patients. He was definitely psychotic but not withdrawn in that sense. As he grinned from ear to ear the piercing look in his eyes told us that he was never truly connected to reality. Sadly he struggled with reality and we all felt that he was somehow teetering on the edge of it at all times, not quite able to cross over. He did have the ability however to hold a basic conversation but it was always interrupted by his sky boxes, rectangles and circles.

There was always something going on around the nursing station. It was the gathering place for the employees as well. Besides the nursing staff and the patients there was always a steady flow of social workers, doctors and program people coming and going. It was a place to confer with people and it was a place to socialize. We sometimes even got a little work done in there as well.

The social workers finish making their phone calls and writing up their follow-up recommendations for the two patients who are leaving today. As soon as the responsible parties arrive to pick them up we will close out their charts. There was a whole procedure that we went through when a patient was admitted or discharged and a ton of paperwork to be filled out, of course. Usually in the next forty-eight to seventy-two hours we will take the charts to medical records to be filed away among the tens of thousands of other charts. Luckily medical records just happened to be located just across the hallway from the unit. All units had to take turns sending nursing staff to medical records to organize and file charts. I used to enjoy that duty believe it or not. It was a welcome break from the commotion of the unit.

It's getting close to lunch time. Food service would always call us when it was time to bring the patients up. Since we had to share the dining room with two other units we didn't always go at the same time. Sometimes they would call us at 11:30 and sometimes it would be 12:30 or later. The dining room had to be cleaned up quickly between groups and the new hot food wheeled into the back kitchen area. All of the hot food dishes were prepared in the main kitchen and taken to the various dining rooms throughout the hospital.

Dr. Ellison wraps up the volleyball game when they call us for lunch and once again we accompany the patients to the dining room. Lunch goes without a hitch today and we bring a few trays back to the unit, one for the newly admitted male patient. Normally I would take 45 minutes to an hour for lunch but today I cheat and gobble down one of the trays we brought back to the unit. We weren't supposed to eat any patient food but there were always some trays left over that were going to get thrown out anyway. I didn't make this a habit however, and usually drove into town to pick up a burger and fries or a burrito somewhere. I rarely brought my own lunch to work because I was never able to get up in time to make it, and making it the night before was just not on my radar screen. Sometimes a group of us would pile into someone's car and hit up the pizza place or the Mexican restaurant.

It's now about 1:30 and I leave the unit to pick up our order from the pharmacy. I have to wait a few minutes until the lady in front of me finishes up. I step up to the counter and say hello to the head pharmacist, Don. Over the years I got to know Don fairly well because we would always exchange small talk, but as a pharmacist he was all business. We go over each item methodically and check them off as we go to make sure that we both agree on the content and the quantities of the order. Everything checks out and I head back to the unit. I take the pharmacy order directly to the medication room and let Jean know that it is here. She will put it all away before midday meds are passed out. Midday meds are not a big deal as there are fewer patients that get meds three times a day. Sometimes if there are not that many the person doing meds that day will take the medication to each patient.

At 2 pm I attend a meeting with the family of one of the patients and the social worker and the doctor. This particular patient is on a two week legal commitment and is scheduled to be discharged in a couple of days. He desperately wants to go home and the family desperately wants him to stay for more treatment. I suggest that if the patient refuses to stay voluntarily then perhaps he would benefit from a day treatment program near his home. The social worker nods in approval. The older brother of the patient snaps in anger and tells me in no uncertain terms that it is not up to me to make those kind of judgement calls. "That is for us and the doctor to decide so I wish you would just stay out of our business!" I say "I'm so sorry, I misspoke. What do you think doctor?" The doctor then went into a long litany about the pros and cons of placing the patient on a temporary conservatorship verses the approach that I had suggested and he definitely agreed that we should try day treatment first. After some more lengthy discussion the family reluctantly agrees to give it a try.

After the family leaves I go back to the nursing station and grab one of the other techs. We then strip down the beds of the discharged patients and clean up the areas. We grab clean sheets, pillowcase and blankets. We all got pretty good at making a perfect hospital bed, with all of the corners tucked precisely just like they taught us in nurses' training. The beds are now ready for new patients to occupy them. The patient population of the unit varied from day to day. We were never 100 percent full but usually had around fifty or sixty patients at any given time. Apparently when the hospital was at its maximum capacity in the 1950's they used to line the hallways with extra beds in order to house the thousands of patients that were being held there.

I then make the rounds to check on everything. I walk down to the recreation room and play a couple of games of ping pong with the patients. I considered myself a fairly good ping pong player at the time so I really had very little competition. That was not the point though and I always made sure that the patients had as much fun as they could. After that I decide to visit some of the patients in the dayroom.

I got into an interesting conversation with a young guy who had been admitted for drug related problems associated with depression and anxiety. He told me about his problem with pills and alcohol and that he had thought of suicide a lot. His drugs of choice were the barbiturates Seconol and Nembutal. "Reds" and "Yellows" were very common on the streets during the 1970's along with methamphetamines and of course psychedelics and marijuana. He said that at one point he was taking so many drugs, and mixing them with large amounts of alcohol, that he almost lost his arm after he had passed out for three days, cutting off the blood supply to it. When he finally woke up his arm was almost black in color and he could not feel it. He went to the emergency room to have his arm looked at and was hospitalized as a result. They were able to save his arm but it did not stop him from his addictions. I tried to relate to him as best I could and listened intently. Of course I gave him words of encouragement and wished him well. I asked him if he thought being here would help him and he said that he felt secure for the time being and was not ready to leave yet.

After I finished up the conversation with that young man I went back to the nurses' station to catch up on some more of my paperwork. I hear some commotion coming from one of the rooms down the hall. Apparently the crazy-eyed man with the beard, who had been sleeping off his #1 injection was wide awake now. So I go down there and Kathy Taylor, one of the techs, is standing by one of the tall lockers with a disgusted look on her face. I look in the open door of the locker and see that this crazy little man had defecated a huge amount in the bottom of it, and it stunk like holy hell. Since there was no air conditioning on the units it tended to be very hot in the summer with only the ventilation of the old metal casement windows and a few electric fans here and there. The heating system was fairly adequate however and kept the unit warm in the cold winter months. Whatever time of year it was didn't really matter, as smells like this seemed to permeate an entire area.

"Where did he go?" I yelled. Kathy said that she saw him run out of the room and vanished somewhere. After a short search we found him in one of the female patients' rooms. He had stripped down completely naked and was bobbing around and making animal like sounds almost like a primate would behave in a zoo. He would inappropriately smile and flash his teeth in between his grunts and chirps. This must have scared the women in that room because they all left abruptly after he wandered in there. I said "OK, I think it's time for another cocktail, don't you Kathy?" "She said "Oh yeah." I called for some back-up and we pinned him down on one of the beds to give him another injection. We then put him back in the side room. We had to medicate this guy around the clock for several days before he started to resemble a human being. By the time he was discharged he was talking, dressing himself, eating properly and was generally cooperative. Sometimes these anti-psychotic drugs really do make a difference.

After that whole fiasco is over and our little friend is resting quietly in the side room, I once again go back to the nursing station and shoot the breeze for a while with some of the other technicians. Some of them are finishing up their charting and Margaret is on the phone in her cubby hole almost oblivious to the rest of the world. It is getting close to the change of shift meeting and I am ready to go home and crack open a few cold beers.

At 3:15 we have a great change of shift meeting with the PM staff, telling them all about the events of the day. Each staff member goes over their patient load and discusses any pertinent information with the oncoming shift. After the meeting the day shift slowly filters off of the unit and into the parking lot. I stop and talk to one of my co-workers for just a second and then climb into my little car. I turn the key, light up a cigarette and crank up the radio station. They are playing "Life in the Fast Lane" by the Eagles, which had just been released. I go home to my wife and have dinner, watch TV and get up the next day to do it all over again. My three day weekend is coming up. Maybe it would be fun to get a few friends together and drive up to the mountains for the day on Saturday. Yes, let's do it!

CHAPTER 9
The Humanity of It

"Men have called me mad; but the question is not yet settled, whether madness is or is not the loftiest intelligence." -Edgar Allan Poe

I would be remiss to say that nothing bothered me or shocked me. There was that initial shock and awe that everyone goes through when you first set foot on one of the units. But, putting that aside, it never ceased to amaze me how even the old timers got thrown for a loop from time to time. It would be impossible for me to write about all of the memorable characters who rotated through the doors of Unit 77 while I was there. Some were so unremarkable and mundane that I would have no recollection of them, but others were electrifyingly insane in their own special way and have been burned into my memory, truly unforgettable. I would like to tell you a few stories about some of the more interesting patients that I had the opportunity to work with. In most cases the old saying "Seeing is believing" does apply but hopefully you can imagine how it might have been to have been there and to have witnessed the strange, the bizarre, the unexplainable and the remarkable side of mankind that we were dealing with.

Before I delve into these interesting and sometimes colorful stories there is another aspect of life in a state hospital that needs to be mentioned. That is the fact that there were certain disgusting conditions and physical manifestations that had to be addressed, and many times were predictably unavoidable.

As a consequence of many patients receiving intra muscular injections they often, over long periods of time, developed what is called a sterile abscess. This almost always occurred in the buttocks in the upper outer quadrant, which is the most commonly used injection site for many anti-psychotic medications, as well as other medications such as Penicillin. The buttock is used because it is a large fleshy area that can more easily absorb liquid injections, especially many of the injections we gave, as they were bigger in volume than say a drug that would be given in the arm. A sterile abscess is really gross to see and I can't imagine how painful and uncomfortable it must have been for the patient. The only saving grace might have been the fact that a lot of the patients who developed sterile abscesses were considered acutely ill or psychotic and usually did not react to pain or discomfort the way a normal person would, nor could they communicate their feelings to you.

Patients who were fairly stable only had to take oral medication but those who were continually agitated or were demonstrating signs of acute psychosis often required a PRN (as needed) to calm them down. PRN's were usually a shot. So as a result the muscle and tissues of the buttocks begin to stop absorbing the liquid medication as it becomes over saturated from too many injections. A large abscess filled with sterile liquid forms in that area. It is hard and tight and is often accompanied by an almost impenetrable scar tissue area around the injection site. The first time I had to give an injection to a patient with a sterile abscess I failed several times before I was able to finally get a needle to penetrate. The needles simply bent or even snapped off. It took the guidance of some of my co-workers who had been doing it for a long time before I developed enough confidence on my own to even attempt it. Many patients unfortunately had abscesses in both butt cheeks. Sometimes we had to use a larger gauge needle and sometimes we were forced to give the injection in other areas of the body, such as the Vastus Lateralis, the large muscle on the top of the thigh. In some cases we had to literally invent new ways to inject patients because their bodies were simply not absorbing any of the medication anymore, rendering it useless.

The anti-psychotic class of drugs we used unfortunately caused severe constipation in many patients. As I stated earlier, mineral oil and laxatives like Dulcolax were frequently given at medication time along with their medications to help prevent this from happening. Even giving the patient an enema didn't always work and it was not uncommon for patients to develop fecal impactions. This could cause illness and physical problems and if not treated could even cause death. Reverse peristalsis, where fecal material comes out of the oral cavity instead of the anus, could even occur. I never saw this but I knew people who had. We had to send several patients to a medical unit for treatment of fecal impactions while I worked there. Not pleasant stuff.

Since the unit itself was a kind of laboratory for every type of infection and communicable disease that you don't want to see, we did. Staph infections were very common and many patients had to be isolated or sent to one of the med/surge units for treatment. Body lice and crabs were another big problem that never seemed to stop floating around the unit. Quell cream was well stocked in the med room and confinement was critical. I remember contracting body lice myself one time and subsequently passing it on to my wife. We both had to apply Quell cream for days to get rid of them. The emphasis was cleanliness, cleanliness, cleanliness but with a revolving door of patients, sometimes consisting of the dregs of mankind, it was virtually impossible to prevent some things from happening. It was part of the job.

I can remember two times that we had a patient die while on the unit. Both of those times I was intimately involved. The first time was when we had admitted an alcoholic on a 5150. He was on a suicide watch ordered by the doctor so we put him in a room next to the nursing station that had an observation window. This was the room where ECT was done and where suicidal patients slept. He had been processed through the main admissions facility very quickly and apparently the admitting doctor had no idea how much he had been drinking and how much was in his system, noting that he had a history of alcoholism and was suicidal.

I had seen several cases of the DT's, even people seeing the proverbial "Pink Elephants" and feeling like they were crawling out of their own skin. We treated these people with Valium and Librium. This man must have had so much alcohol in his system and had been drinking so much just prior to his admission that he not only showed the classic symptoms of withdrawal, such as seeing things and picking at things, but he went into the DT's soon after his arrival. We were watching him very closely. I was personally doing the required 15 minute check on him when I noticed that he was not breathing. I called for immediate help and several people came running in. We performed CPR and chest compressions on him until the fire department arrived. I can still remember the horrible sound of ribs breaking as his chest was being violently compressed by the fire department in a valiant effort to save his life, but it was too late. He died.

The other time was when I was working the evening shift and shower time was just finishing. There was a male patient using one of the two bathtubs we had. I was in the nursing station and two of the other male techs had been overseeing the shower room. This patient was considered a potential suicide risk as well but I don't believe he was on Q15 checks ordered by the doctor. Somehow the patient was left alone in the shower room for a brief period of time. He had taken several towels and tied them together around his neck and around the faucet on the bathtub. He sank down into the water and effectively drowned himself. It was really quick. Another patient, who had just gone in there, slowly and nonchalantly walked down to the nursing station and informed me that there was a "dead man floating in the bathtub." I ran as fast as I could to the shower room and pulled the patient out of the water and onto the floor. He was blue and not breathing. I began mouth to mouth resuscitation and in the process the patient aspirated his own vomit into my mouth. I cleared out his mouth and continued CPR. It was to no avail. The patient, I'm sure, was dead before the fire department arrived. They tried all the life saving measures they could, but he was dead. There was a massive incident report as a result. No one got in any serious trouble as it was viewed as an unfortunate incident at the time. I received a letter of commendation from the fire department for my valiant attempt to save his life.

We had a few very close calls as well. It is always a good feeling when you know you did your very best to save a life. When we were a co-ed unit we had an overweight, very crazy, wild patient named Lois who was unpredictable and a real handful. She seemed to agitate everyone around her at all times and needed to be heavily medicated. She continued to act out even with the tranquilizers. She was not suicidal per se, rather an extreme attention getter. She somehow managed to get ahold of some matches and locked herself in one of the stalls in the ladies restroom. I just happened to be walking by there as I was coming back from one of the doctor's offices when I heard her screaming and could see smoke coming from the stall. She had lit herself on fire. She had been wearing one of those plain, brown hospital dresses issued by the state, which I'm sure was very flammable.

I yelled out loudly "Fire"! I tried to open the stall but it was locked. I scaled the walls of the stall and landed next to her. I unlocked the stall door and threw her on the floor. She was engulfed in flames. I grabbed some towels to try to put the fire out about the same time two of the female technicians arrived. I said to find some rugs, anything. They came running back with a couple of rugs from the doctor's offices and we rolled her up in them, extinguishing the fire. She suffered severe burns on her body but recovered, in time. I was again awarded a certificate of merit by the fire department.

We had many patients who suffered from seizures and brain disorders. Phenobarbital, Dilantin and other drugs were used to control epileptic seizures in most patients. I only saw status epilepticus occur once. This is where a person goes into a seizure for a long period of time, over five minutes. This seizure was the tonic-clonic type, with a regular pattern of contraction and extension of the arms and legs. This patient went into status and he would not stop seizing. This can be life threatening if not controlled. We called the doctor into the room immediately and he tried certain drugs that would not stop the seizures. As a last resort he ordered IV Diazepam or "Valium". Diazepam was rarely used intravenously, at least it wasn't at Camarillo State Hospital. It worked. The seizures stopped. The patient lived to see another day.

There were all elements of mankind represented in the patient population. To say that we had our share of disgusting, putrid and hopelessly pathetic people pass through our doors would be an understatement. Some of these people were so terrible in the way they looked and the way they acted that it was very hard to believe that they could in anyway be a benefit to society. How they came to be the way they were was a mystery in many cases. A lot of them had very little information in their charts about their past history, where that came from or how they might have survived up to this point. Some, on the other hand, were equally disgusting but had been in the system for a long time and just kept bouncing from one facility to another; jail, the streets, board and care, county, state hospital etc. We took them in and we fed them and clothed them and tried, in mostly vain attempts, to package them into something they were not.

I'm sure you have heard of, or have seen, extremely dirty, disheveled people on the street or in a public setting somewhere. You think to yourself "That is the dirtiest person I have ever seen". Well I can truly say that we had a patient on Unit 77 who was without a doubt the dirtiest, slimiest, most infested looking individual that we had ever seen. No one knew where he came from. He did not talk much, just mumbled. He looked like he had crawled out of a cave. He had hair down to his waist and a full beard about two feet long. His clothes were so old and soiled that they were literally fused onto his body, they were shiny black with dirt. His hair was so matted and tangled that no shampoo would ever get it clean. There were lice and fleas living all over his body. He only had a few teeth in his head. He was a white man but it was hard to tell. The dirt was imbedded into his skin. You could see the whites of his eyes peering out from the filth. He had no identification, no money, only a few things in his pockets. He was skin and bones. What do you do with someone like this?

It took us hours to cut the clothes off of him, shave his beard off, shave his head, and scrub his skin in the shower. The dirt and mud ran down the drain for an eternity. Even after he had been on the unit for several weeks, and had been getting a thorough scrubbing in the shower every day, the dirt was still embedded in his skin. He began eating after much coaxing and was finally able to tell us his name. That was about it. He was eventually transferred to a long term unit. We did what we could for him but I don't think he really appreciated it. He would have been happy to have never been brought in there in the first place.

Icky Scats was another wanton, vile man that we saw on several occasions. I don't think that was his real name but that is what he went by and that is what it said in his chart. He had been hospitalized many times and was known to most of us. He was partially paralyzed and walked with a tormented limp, as he dragged his body around from place to place. He only stood about four feet eight inches tall. There was absolutely no grace within this man. His vitriolic nature was renowned throughout the M.I. side of the hospital. He was extremely disheveled and filthy with greasy hair and horribly bad breath. His disposition was that of an angry, putrid psychotic wreck who would just as soon spit on you as look at you. When he spoke in his rough, throaty voice it was a solid stream of insults to anyone who was around him, interrupted by coughing, drooling, choking and spitting. He would literally soil himself right in front of you and laugh about it. I don't know whatever happened to him, and I don't care.

Psychology books might contain classic examples, or "textbook" examples of specific types of mental illness.

It is true that there are common behaviors used to describe Classic Schizophrenia. Over the years certain movies and books have enlightened people's knowledge of these strange individuals. When I first began my training to become a psych tech I spent time on Unit 20, one of the long term units that had many of these "Classic" patients.

One of those patients I remember fondly. I'll just call him Jesse, and anyone who worked at the hospital during those years would know of him. Jesse was a long-time resident of Camarillo State Hospital; it was his home. He had been studied by scores of psychiatrists, researchers and psych students for decades. He was for all intents and purposes the most classic, textbook example of Schizophrenia Classic Undifferentiated Type that anyone had ever seen. I was introduced to Jesse on the first day I was on Unit 20. It was amazing to see him in person. It was thrilling in a way. If you were to open a book describing the behavior of these people he would check every box. His reality was truly split, he was fully psychotic.

He could not carry on a conversation with you but he could speak, especially when he wanted or needed something, such as a cigarette. He called cigarettes "empty sickrocks". He spoke word salad, a so called separate language made up of nonsensical, disconnected words and phrases that is associated with classic schizophrenia. He mostly sat in a chair smoking one cigarette after another and drinking coffee out of the same old coffee stained cup. His fingers were deeply stained with tobacco tar, as he would smoke every cigarette down to the filter and light another one. He would rock back and forth for hours in his chair. Sometimes he would get up and walk around the unit, never making eye contact with anyone. If you approached him he would look away. He walked almost sideways with a bizarre and inappropriate posture. When you could see his eyes you could tell there was nothing in there. He was in his own world, permanently separated from reality. He demonstrated the classic self-stimming finger movements where he would hold his hands in front of his face and wiggle his fingers. He would stare at his fingers as they were twiddling rapidly before his eyes. About the only socialization skill that he had was to form a coy little smile out of the side of his mouth if he was confronted by someone, usually a staff member. He was cute in a way, a novelty. He was completely harmless. His mannerisms and behavior were unforgettable. Everyone loved him but no one could reach him.

After I left the hospital to pursue other endeavors I never forgot about Jesse. He was one of a kind. There were many other patients who were just as psychotic, but none that exhibited so many classic behaviors in one person. I don't know what happened to Jesse. I hope he found a new home in another institution, where he could live out his remaining years and retain some sense of happiness and security. If there is a God up there, Jesse would be blessed.

I can think of many strange cases that I encountered over the years on Unit 77. There was the man who had destroyed his mind by inhaling gasoline fumes. He was basically a vegetable when we received him. He had about as much left in his general cognition as someone with a lobotomy. Instead of craving "brains" like a zombie would he craved gas fumes. He managed to escape one day and we knew where to find him. We searched the parking lot near the unit to find him kneeling in front of an open gas cap inhaling as many fumes as he could. We returned him to the unit and he spent the remainder of his days there pacing around like a wild animal in an effort to find an escape route so he could run directly to the first car he found.

We had a number of gay and lesbian patients that revolved through our doors who carried with them their own unique set of problems. We not only had gay patients with severe emotional problems but we had transgender and transsexual patients as well, even in the mid 1970's. Many of these people struggled with their own identities, as they tended to dress strangely and often had strange hair styles for the time. Many wore makeup and some colored their hair in bright purple, green or pink shades. What is a common place lifestyle now was definitely not as socially accepted then. Their behavior was sometimes characterized by fits of anger, temper tantrums, uncontrollable crying or inappropriate criticism of others around them. They also could suffer from depression and anxiety and many were suicidal. Minor tranquilizers, mood elevators and group and individual therapy were the treatment methods of choice.

We had a patient whose diagnosis was "Mania". This is a fairly rare condition in that it is similar to bi-polar or manic depressive illness but the person only stays in the manic phase, rather than going from up to down and down to up. The patient is always high or manic and never comes down. In this case the patient lived up to his diagnosis. Unless he was heavily sedated he would race around the unit at light speeds, never settling down for just one minute, constantly talking and moving his arms and head around in a thousand positions. Remarkably Mania was sometimes treated with Benzedrine, a powerful stimulant, as it somehow caused a paradoxical effect in the brain, calming the patient down. As far as I can remember he did respond to the medication and was able to let his body rest, at least for a while.

A very young male patient was admitted to the unit one time who looked completely normal for his age, had a nice personality, and was actually very handsome, except for one thing, he couldn't stop shaking. He shook and trembled, sometimes violently, from the time he got up in the morning until the time he went to bed at night.

He could barely hold a glass of water it was so bad. Of course he was given medication to reduce the shaking and calm his nervous system but it did not stop it altogether. This severe condition, that caused him to shake so badly, was never really pin-pointed while he was there. The doctors could not find any physical causation and suspected it was psychosomatic in nature. I really think that if it were not for the shaking he would have had a chance of being a normal, well-adjusted person. I personally spent hours talking to him and he could offer no explanation of why he was that way. It apparently started when he was a very young adult and continued to get worse. Whether it was a result of problems growing up or peer pressure or just a fear of fitting in, was unknown. He did experience anxiety but it was unclear whether the anxiety caused the shaking or the shaking caused the anxiety. He told me how he so desperately wanted to date girls and hang out with the guys, but because of his disorder he was forced to shy away. He was discharged from the unit and I never saw him again. I really hope he was able to grow out of it.

Steven was a fifty year old man that stood over six feet tall but acted like a small child or even an infant. He literally made "goo-goo and gaga" noises. This psychotic symptom, even though it is well documented, is fairly uncommon in the way it manifests itself in an individual. I only recall seeing a couple of cases like this. He had the mannerisms and vocabulary of a two year old but could eat an incredible amount of food, even though he was very slender. We had to limit him in the dining room because he would not stop eating. He would literally go from table to table and grab food off of other patients' plates if he was left unsupervised. He would eat until his stomach was so packed with food it resembled that of a person with a severe case of abdominal distention. He was chronically ill and probably spent the rest of his life in an institution.

We admitted a woman who came in on a 5150 that had previously been a career social worker and a highly respected professional. She had no prior history of mental illness but for some reason began to unravel in front of her family, her clients, and her co-workers. By the time she was admitted to our unit she had become completely agitated, displaying an inappropriate, loquacious affect and was acting in lewd and promiscuous ways. I can't say that she was psychotic, just that she was out of her mind. Her family came to visit her and they were very shocked to see her that way. The second or third day she walked into the nursing station as I was doing some paperwork and started laughing and pacing around frantically. She then raised her arms up in the air and said "Come piss with me!" That really caught my attention. She was placed on a two week hold after the 5150 and with the aid of the medication slowly returned to normal.

Then there were the amazing psychotic twins, Albert and William. They were identical twins in their late twenties who had been in and out of the hospital countless times. It seemed like we either had one or the other on the unit at all times, sometimes both at the same time. They were both considered borderline as they would slip in and out of psychosis, and when they did it was severe enough to land them in the hospital again. They were always highly agitated upon admission and would be in a crisis mode. Although their parents were not psychotic they both had mental issues of their own. It was like a three ring circus when they would converge on the unit. Sometimes they would bring William with them when they visited Albert and vice versa, always causing problems for everyone concerned. Every time one of them was admitted the whole staff would cringe because we knew what was in store for us.

I could go on and on with stories about the mentally ill and disabled people that my co-workers and I treated during those critical years in the history of Camarillo State Hospital. I have a thousand more stored somewhere in my memory. There are many rumored or substantiated accounts of celebrities and famous people being hospitalized there. I could drop a few names, but I won't. So hopefully you now have a better understanding of what it was like for us and for the patients themselves, as the so-called world of insanity collided with the world of normality. A strange environment indeed, but a necessary one in my opinion.

The environment on the unit and the manner in which the patients interacted with themselves and with the staff was a complex arrangement in its own right. Given the wide variety of conditions, personalities and emotions that were present at any given time it somehow fit together like the world's most difficult jigsaw puzzle. One thing would feed off of another in a dizzying merry-go-round of human agony, conflict, confusion and hope. It still amazes me how I made it through those years physically unscathed. Mentally? I think my mind and senses are intact, however the recurring dream that I had for many years after I left the hospital about waking up in a mental hospital as a patient still haunts me to this day.

Throughout the history of psychiatric hospitals in this country and abroad there has been much debate about their worth, their effectiveness and their morality. Many of these hospitals were indeed infamous. Rumors of patients climbing the walls and being tortured, beaten, raped, neglected and experimented on were omnipresent. It was assumed that these unfortunate souls were simply locked away and forgotten about. There were scores of unreported "mysterious deaths". Many people walked the halls of these dark institutions as if their minds had been removed from them, the result of seemingly senseless and cruel lobotomies. The terms "lunatic asylum" and "insane asylum" were often used. It wasn't until the early 1950's, when the era of psychotropic drugs was ushered in, that the connotations surrounding mental hospitals began to change for the better. Dementia Praecox, or Schizophrenia, could now be treated much more effectively and a lot of the old methods were abandoned. Chlorpromazine, or Thorazine as it is known in the U.S., was the first antipsychotic drug discovered around 1950, followed by many others. The combination of treating patients with this new class of drugs, and groundbreaking psychotherapy techniques, basically revolutionized the science of dealing with mental illness and the attempt to improve the mental health of many thousands of people.

And yes, we saw it all. We saw the psychotic, the neurotic, the manic-depressive, the alcoholic, the depressed, the addicted, the drug induced, the brain injured, the epileptic, and the developmentally disabled. We saw people with virtually every described mental illness, disability and diagnosis. We saw people briefly and we saw them virtually their whole lives. We fought with them and we comforted them. We feared them and we controlled them. We laughed with them and we cried with them. We saw progress and we saw complete failure. We saved them from self-destruction and we reveled in their self-realizations. We cleaned their wounds and bandaged their cuts. We bathed them and we dressed them and we fed them. We cared deeply for many of them. That was Unit 77 in the 1970's.

CONCLUSION

I am now in my mid-sixties. I completely left the mental health field in 1979 and followed a different path in life. I am happily retired and finally have enough time on my hands to dabble in some of the things I always wanted to do. One of them was to write a book about my experiences at Camarillo State Hospital in the 1970's. When I decided to write it I didn't know if I could remember enough of the details, but as I began to jot things down it became clearer and clearer. The result was, in my opinion, a very factual account of what really went on in that famous place and in that important time.

Volumes have been written about the conditions and the treatment methods used at mental institutions and there is no doubt that there is a negative connotation associated with them. Camarillo State Hospital was no exception. There has always been that element, that element of the unknown, and the dark seedy nature of mental illness itself. Going way back to the conceptualization of the first institutions in Europe in the early 1800's, and the historical evolution of them that took place there and in the United States, the perpetuation of societal attitudes has continued to this day.

The truth is that things did happen there, at Camarillo State Hospital, be them good or bad. I am not going to judge however, as the whole grand experiment will fade away into the future, remembered only in the pages of dusty books. Who knows how mental illness will be treated in the decades or centuries to come. Maybe they will discover an amazing cure for it, but probably not. I'm mostly proud of what we were trying to do in those days. Do I have any regrets? Some. Would I do it all over again? Probably not. I did then and I still do now have a special place reserved in my heart for all of the people who have been caught in the grip of these devastating illnesses. Sometimes I wonder, if it were at all possible, that perhaps their souls remain behind, pacing back and forth throughout the corridors of those old, all knowing buildings.

So as I climbed into my car on the last day of my employment I realized that the familiar set of keys was no longer hanging off my belt. I left the grounds for the last time and snaked through the winding road that leads to the freeway. I glanced back for just a second as an existential thought washed over me. What a rush!

I sincerely hope that you gained something from reading my perspective. Thank you for your time.

"The mind is everything. What you think, you become." - Buddha

72608950R00092